Celebration

What our lives can truly be

ISBN: 1497597293
ISBN 13: 9780692599372

1

A Joyous Birth

March 20th, 1950, the day had come. Celebration abounded with the birth of Angela Jane Morgan. This celebration exceeded the view and imaginations of her elated and grateful young family. Above and beyond the hospital room filled with laughter and excitement, all crowded around mother and newborn, a celebration was taking place of unimaginable proportions.

In a dimension the family could not see, angels rejoiced at the birth of this extraordinary child who had just come into the world, sent to be a shining example, as others had been sent before her. The scene exploded with color and sound, voices beautiful and melodious filling the entire landscape as far as could be seen. The angels themselves were magnificent, pure white which exploded from them in lines of brilliant light, streaming out from their forms, mixed with dazzling colors, in all directions, filling the area and beyond the horizon unending. These colors in the midst of the blinding white emanations flashed into view and then suddenly were gone. Your eyes searching for it, desiring to hold it, and then not being there, but in startling fashion replaced by another in a marvelous dance beyond any ever seen.

They sang of the child's qualities, ones that she would show and live so well. They sang of how she would brighten wherever she went, illuminating the scene with the power of her presence. They told of how people would be drawn to her, wanting to be around her, and how they would be changed by the encounter.

They sang of how all people are precious, containing within them this same potential to live as this child will, but many not attaining it. Angela Jane Morgan will do this and shine like a small sun to the world and they will bask in the warmth, and her light, and in her spirit.

The angels knew of the great gifts that each person carries within them to this world, and when fully expressed how they are a wonderful and powerful thing; ignored, and they are a great loss of potential and joy for others. The celebration rang loud because here is one who will express all of the gifts given to her, and will show others the way if they will follow.

2

A Flower Blooms

Angela did indeed express all of the great love of life and love for others she had, just as the angels sang about. She never seemed to lose her childlike wonder and enthusiasm for her world either. She was always taken by the smallest things, these wonderful details that never lost their appeal and novelty to her. One day, at the age of three, she was outside playing in the dirt as her mother planted flowers. The wind suddenly began to pick up. Angela rose and stood tall, arms outstretched as it enveloped her. She smiled and closed her eyes, and then began to turn and call out in joy.

Even at age three she told her mother that her favorite sound of all was the sound of the wind as it passes through pine trees. She tried to describe it to her mother, standing up, arms raised, swaying and making a long, soft, swishing sound.

When she was old enough she loved to walk down to an area near her house. It was a very tall hill that looked down over a big park, and the hill was lined with thick pine trees all along the top. The spot was well hidden by the great trees, hiding her on her perch high above the park. She said then that this serene high point made her soul rise and felt great energy from the experience. She waited in anticipation and then the wind would rise and it would build, and then pass though. She would listen eagerly to the sound as it hit the line of trees on the hill. First the wind would strike the trees furthest away on this hill she loved so dear, and then it would make its' way closer and closer. It would then hit, and pass through, filling her spirit.

She also loved looking up at the tallest of pines she could find. First marveling at their seemingly endless height, which always made her feel dizzy, almost falling down. Then, she would wait and listen for the wind to pass through which added to the grandeur of their great height.

She would go home and describe it all with great excitement to her mother, who was always amazed by what her daughter would come home and say. Fortunately her mother kept record of many of the things that Angela said. In one instance she recorded at age 5 her saying,

"Mommy. Why does it seem as though no one notices all the beauty around them? I never hear them talk about it? How can they miss it?"

"I don't know dear", her mother answered.

"I just can't understand. It's all so close, and so overwhelming, and everyday it's different. I see something I never noticed before."

"Maybe you're here to show them," her mother told her with a smile, and picked Angela up and kissed her.

"That would be great fun, she said."

"Yes it would," her mother agreed.

That same year, not too long after her conversation at home with her mother Angela asked her teacher at school if they could all play a game. Her teacher had grown to be very enamored with her and was very curious what it was that she wanted to do.

Angela turned to face the class and said,

"Who would like to fly?!"

Everyone answered loudly all throughout the room with a resounding yes.

"I would love to play a game where we all "fly" though our world around us."

Angela turned to her teacher, "Is that okay?" Her teacher agreed.

She turned on the stereo they had for the classroom. It began to play the song, "The Age of Aquarius," by the Fifth Dimension. The teacher had never heard the song before and looked curiously at the stereo.

Angela then called to all the class to follow her and go flying. The children trusted her and always became excited over Angela's infectious spirit. She began by leading all the kids with arms outstretched through their class, swirling and turning in a tight line that didn't break even as they wove their way through the classroom. All of the children were laughing as they went, arms outstretched together, as the music played. The teacher stood in dumb amazement at the unity and joy the children were showing. Then the music rose louder. The teacher again stared at the stereo in bewilderment.

The door was open and Angela led the whole class out and into the hallway of the school. Her teachers jaw dropped as they streamed out of the classroom door and out in the hallway before she could realize what was happening.

In the hallway the excitement mounted. The music was now playing all through the P.A. system and all of the kids were laughing and staying tightly together as they made their way through the hall of the school. Other kids caught the spirit and seeing what was happening, came running out of their classrooms, their teachers calling out behind them. Nothing could slow it down, but it was a joyous, good spirited moment, the children joined in unison in a seemingly effortless flight, through the school, more adding to their number as they passed the classrooms.

Kids rushed to their door to see what all the commotion was, others just running out of open classroom doors and joining the line. It happened so fast and was so unique the teachers stood watching, mouths open and eyes wide.

This wondrous event was aided by the Angels who rejoiced at Angela's birth, working through her childlike wonder and excitement in a display of supernatural power by providing the accompanying music. This would announce the beginning of Angela's using her potential to influence the world. This song and the triumphant line of children with her would signify its start.

All of the children had their arms out wide and straight and no one broke the unity of the line. The music fit so perfectly and fueled the kids on and definitely gave the perfect air for the scene. The timing was perfect as the song went into the part singing about letting the sun shine. The huge line burst through the open front doors of the school as a delivery was coming in. The men quickly got out of the way for the massive procession, eyes wide in disbelief.

"What the hell?!" One of the men called out as he turned to get out of the way of the kids, arms overhead.

Another man looked up at the speakers trying to understand why they were playing the song loudly, and one that no one had ever heard before.

The grand procession made its' way out the door of the school and began to go around the large fountain in front, which was spraying a huge spout of water out of the top. The children stayed in their tight line, the music playing loudly still, heard through loudspeakers designed for announcements. Some of the children were catching the repeated chorus and singing as loudly as they could, repeating the lines about the sun and letting it shine.

Angela led the children to hold hands and side step their way around the fountain as the music continued to play. Many teachers were at the top of the stairway out front of the school watching them go around and around; some shaking their heads, some laughing, others clapping.

The music stopped, the children laughing and carrying on joyfully, then walking right back up the stairs and into the school as if they just had a normal recess period. This made the teachers even more dumbstruck than what had just happened, silent and moving out of the way as the children filed past them, all going to their classrooms in a totally orderly fashion.

Her mother was at the school shortly after, having been called by the principal. He was livid. The office staff were all smiles as he was heard talking to Angela's mother behind his office door, more upset by a seeming loss of control than anything else, not phased by the joy and unity of the children.

Needless to say, there was not, unfortunately so, another incident like the one that day for quite some time. And despite the principal's displeasure over it Angela's spirit was never to be squelched. She kept her zeal for life and the world around her and still infected all those around her to feel the same, but at her mother's behest, displayed a little differently.

All was quiet in her class after the "flying incident," as their stodgy principal liked to call it, still not seeing any of the beauty in what happened. It sadly had just bounced off him. Angela's spirit would have no effect on him at all, he was insulated from it, not allowing such "silly thoughts" to ever enter his head. Some of the teachers though were amused by what happened, others saw Angela as a charismatic leader. But some were struck by a love for life and a freedom and joy they had never seen before, and were stirred to seek that for their own lives.

At this time Angela was deeply absorbed in a project at home, that perhaps being the reason it was so quiet around the school. She had been about the business of catching butterflies. In their yard her mother had created an amazing and very large garden. With all of the flowers her mother planted and all of the bountiful amounts of flowering plants indigenous to their own area, it all made for an area thick with bees and also with butterflies. Angela wanted to catch as many as she could. She asked her if it would be okay to house them temporarily, so her mother built her a huge sanctuary for them to live in. Angela wanted to honor them, by gathering them, appreciating their beauty and then releasing them back to the world where they belong. She was elated by their beauty, wanted to "honor it," and then have them fly out in a magnificent moment, "Showing what they bring to the world," she said.

Her mother had been so busy that she had not had the time to really follow the progress of her little girl's project. One afternoon her mother heard Angela working outside talking with the butterflies, and went out to see. Her mother could not believe how many there were. "How did she do it?", she thought.

Although her mother had managed to be amazed by her daughter before, she found that she was constantly discovering how much more there was to her all the time.

Angela saw her mother coming out. "Aren't they beautiful?"

"Yes, very much so." Her mother answered.

"They're ready for their glorious show." Angela announced.

"Show?"

"Yes, where they will be admired and then soar on their glorious way back to their homes."

"Where were you planning to do that honey?"

"At school. In the atrium. I love that place. That way they can be seen up close as we circle around them. Then when they are released, and sent back home, they can fly up together through the tunnel, and then when they hit the sky at the top they will spread out on their way!" She jumped up, arms raised as she finished.

Her mother couldn't believe her 6 year old daughter thought of this. She really wanted to facilitate her daughter's unique gifts, but wondered how she would be able to work this out so it could be done at the school. She felt some concern for her daughter though because as wonderful as her idea was she was afraid her principal would shut it down right away. She thought of his reaction after the "flying" incident.

"Her teacher," her mother thought, "Her teacher would understand. Her teacher did let her lead the class out of the room that day."

The next day her mother went to the teacher to talk to her about the butterfly release. Her teacher agreed thinking it was a great idea and wanted to help. She formulated a plan to make it happen. She thought of circumventing the principal by taking her class down to the atrium and having Angela's mom drop off the butterfly keep there, since it is right off the drive in front of the school, and then they could release them and come back to class.

The next day the teacher had the class waiting in the atrium at the designated time. The atrium, as it was called by the school, was a small alcove at the edge of the school building. It was attached to the beautiful old red brick school, a circular patio as it were, designed to be a small courtyard with a skylight, having high curved walls leading to an open top where you could see the sky, and a curved bench for seating at the bottom around the edge. It was truly perfect for what Angela wanted to do, her mother and teacher couldn't stop marveling at the imagination of the idea.

Her mother was so excited but also nervous as she pulled up with the large pen full of butterflies in her truck at the school that morning. The class was patiently waiting in the atrium with the teacher, not knowing what they were waiting for. Angela's mother and her boyfriend unloaded the large wooden cage and carried it into the atrium. The kids gasped as they saw it. Angela was all smiles, beaming from ear to ear. They placed the pen right in the middle of the small area, the bright blue sky directly above it at the top.

The teacher stepped up as Angela asked her to, not wanting to draw attention upon herself, and explained to the class why all these butterflies are here. Her teacher went on to explain to the class how all these butterflies were caught by someone anonymously, so we could appreciate them and their great beauty, and then we could send them soaring together as they should be, free.

She had the kids quietly walk closer to take in the splendor of the butterflies. The whole class slowly and carefully approached the large pen. They were all amazed by the combination of powerfully bright colors and movement of them which mixed and blended the colors and patterns marvelously together in that space.

The teacher pulled the string to release the top of the pen and the butterflies started to fly out of the open top. They then all swirled up and filled the circular atrium walls thickly in a kaleidoscope of motion and color, flying tightly together and out of the open top where they spread out spectacularly to the sun and sky.

There was an exchange of gasps and cute small voices all chiming in excitedly as it happened. The kids started to jump up and down as the butterflies all flew out together in a wide stream. The children celebrated, jumping and clapping, after it was over. Angela's mom hugged her teacher and thanked her for making this all possible.

In the years that followed Angela visited her kindergarten teacher often and many times brought her cut flowers from their garden. She never forgot how her teacher supported her and nurtured her that year. But she knew her greatest supporter was her mother. She would marvel and laugh to herself thinking of how they let her do that with the butterflies. Now that she was older she felt so grateful that her mother didn't squelch her. She had a special feeling for her mother because of all she did and who she was, a warmth and gratitude she would never be able to fully express. She wanted to devote her life to doing that for others as her mother did for her, feeling deeply to never squelch another person's dreams, but to be there to lift and grow their spirit. That became her life's mantra, blossoming out of her mother's careful handling of her.

She grew, and continued in the same spirit fortunately as when she was little. She never lost that childlike wonder for life. Now a teenager in high school she still retained those same qualities. It was a good era for her to be in, 1960's America, as this was a great time for her to flourish. It was a time of introspection, and call for change, for appreciation of the environment and living in harmony with it, and of free spirits. Angela did flourish well in this decade, indeed the perfect time for her to be here. She loved philosophy, poetry, and music, and was very interested in influencing public policy. She was very involved in the spirit of change, and believed we could make the world a better place, if we all did this together.

She was so physically attractive that the boys of her school totally clamored to get her attention. They fell over themselves trying to win her over. She had a powerful personality and zest for life that made her even more alluring. Her clothes matched her beauty and personality. She dressed in the bright, flamboyant colors of the decade; bright patterned pants, and shirts that matched in color and flair. She had no interest however in these boys who were captivated by her looks. She saw through their shallowness and would be literally repelled by them. Young men like that lived in a different world, almost universe to her, compared to what occupied her thoughts. Life to her was a pursuit of self-improvement, of harmony with the world, and of nature. She had a great desire to learn and to grow.

So the boys were all left frustrated and bewildered by this young lady who so strongly and vividly stood out among her peers, and lamented over how all of their machinations which had made them famous with the ladies before all failed miserably with Angela. She had friends that were boys but none she could think of romantically. I think at times she doubted that she had a true kindred spirit out there. But as she always did, she remained hopeful.

3

Angels on the Rooftop

Several miles away from the town where Angela lived, Ethan Brown was peering out his bedroom window. He spent time with his friends as most teenage boys his age do but he also loved spending a lot of time by himself. He loved to read and was very introspective, thinking about life and our purpose for being here. He also wanted to find the real meaning of his existence and see a bigger picture. He couldn't settle for the mundane things that occupied most people's minds. He felt odd sometimes comparing what mattered to him to what seemed to drive everyone else. This made him feel alone and somewhat isolated from the other kids at school. But in his inner most being he knew this is who he was and couldn't change that, and upon reflection, would never want to.

He knew there was more to life and thought a lot about it, but his dilemma was he didn't know how to get there. It occupied a lot of his time, it had his attention but he didn't know what direction to go to attain it. It was starting to frustrate him a bit. But he wouldn't quit in his pursuit. He knew there was more. The kids he knew seemed to be only concerned with what other people thought of them, and what they were doing this weekend. It began to occupy his thoughts more and more and the feeling to do something about it grew within him. But again his dilemma was that he didn't really know what to do.

He used to love to go onto his roof for contemplation and meditation. It was his way to get away and get close to nature around him and try and seek his answers. The house was very tall, and felt to Ethan that it reached high into the sky. He would go out on the large flat roof which was just below the top slanted roof. His neighborhood had large trees that flowed from yard to yard and covered most of the roads as well. They created a wonderful landscape with them at the forefront. They dominated and created a great feeling when you were among them. Ethan loved to be on the roof and watch the great tall trees sway in the wind, the sound powerfully rising like a great throng of people cheering together. This would enter his soul every time and he would just bask in the sound and the feeling. He never tired of it and always felt great energy enter him through the power of the wind and great sound it made. This was one of his favorite spots to be. When he was there he felt most alive, but wanted that though wherever he went. He wondered if that was possible? He made it his quest to find out.

He began to pray about his thoughts. As the wind blew he began to ask to know more about life and how to feel closer to his world and how to live on a higher plane. He felt as though he was speaking to the whole universe that day in his prayer. The wind seemed to almost drown out his thoughts but he loved the feeling. The great sound of it felt like a powerful accompaniment to his prayers. As he continued it seemed to Ethan that his message was traveling much further than where he was and that he was being heard.

The sun was beginning to beam light though the mass of trees as it started to go down high up on his perch, upon his roof spot. This day though it seemed to grow in intensity instead of how it usually diminishes. The usual soft radiant glow streaming through the trees, that always made his soul rise, kept growing in intensity as he watched. The light continued to grow and then finally feel as though it was moving towards him. He looked down for an instant and as he looked back up the light was all around him, enveloping the area with a warm, soft glow. It seemed to cover everything. He couldn't see past the soft, diffuse light that had covered him and his rooftop sanctuary. He felt a warmth and euphoric feeling he had never felt before. This radiance seemed to swirl around him and it made him feel as though he were moving. He heard a voice speak in his mind, greeting him.

"Who are you?" He thought.

There was no answer.

Then, he heard a voice again say to him, "What you seek can be found. What you search for you can attain. Don't falter from your pursuit. You will find your way."

"How?" Ethan thought.

He was still so overwhelmed he was having trouble focusing on what the voice was telling him. But as the moments passed he was able to focus and relax and admire the beauty of what was around him and trust it as well.

"I want to learn."

"You will," He heard in his mind. "Stay on your path. Listen. Be open to what is around you and it will present itself to you. It will all come."

He sensed the light was leaving, and their time was ending.

"Wait," He thought. There are so many things I want to ask you."

"Stay steadfastly on your path. You will discover what you seek."

"Wait! Don't Go."

Then he sensed, "You must discover this yourself. Nothing should rob you of the joy of that discovery."

Then the words in his thoughts were gone and the light had vanished.

After nearly twenty minutes he realized he was standing in the same spot, unmoved. Startled at the realization, he began to try and make sense of it all.

He was so motivated by what happened, feeling confirmation that he was right, that there was more. His inner feeling that most people are chasing after the wrong things was right. He felt his thoughts had been validated. He wasn't alone anymore. His soul felt so solidified. Ethan had thought that he was strange and felt beat down from the world and how differently he felt about life. Even his parents told him to get his head out of the clouds and wouldn't allow him to share his thoughts about it anymore.

The angels', as he thought of them, act of kindness and compassion deeply affected him. It also made him feel like he wanted to dedicate himself to helping others feel the same. He thought that receiving such a great blessing made him want to be a blessing to others. Their support so comforted him that Ethan wanted to be able to return it to people in kind, a tribute to Ethan that those were his initial thoughts after such a visitation.

He longed for someone else who shared this feeling about life, that he could safely tell his experience to. He couldn't imagine a person like that now, or anyone feeling the way he did about things, but as with everything else, he always had hope.

4

New School

Angela used to get to school early every morning so she could spend quiet time in her favorite spot on the edge of the school grounds. Their school used to be a tremendous estate owned by a wealthy family that eventually donated it all to the town for a school. It had beautiful rolling hills of bright green grass and tall trees all around. She especially loved her spot at the top of one of the hills with trees surrounding it, creating a cozy closed in sanctuary for her to have privacy and peace. She would go there before school every morning and sit before it started, taking in the scene and looking out to this area that she loved so. She would raise her head looking high up into the trees and again listen for her favorite sound, the wind through the tall pine trees. Sometimes she would close her eyes and listen to the sound and feel the breeze run across her, brushing by and greeting her as she called it, feeling it raise her spirit. The soft breezes that blew that morning calmed her and soothed her. The stronger winds that also blew that morning energized her, and she loved to feel their power. She sat feeling as though she was absorbing the energy from it, the power feeling transferred into her.

It made her think back of a trip to visit friends in the Pacific Northwest and how she would go for long walks even though it was winter. Because it was so cold no one went with her. She walked down to the shoreline and marveled at the beauty of the frost on the round gray rocks that lined the shore there. She turned and looked out over the water, it was all eerily and wonderfully quiet due to it being winter. "Every season has its positives," she thought. She remembered how after that she climbed up off the shoreline and walked into an open field near a thick wooded area. Then, seeing mist flowing through that field captivated her attention. It was like a cloud floating just above the ground. She followed it and watched as it met the trees of the dark forest in its' path, melding with the trees as it pressed in and then disappeared.

As the wind picked up where she was now she remembered on that same trip standing on the shore at the Straights of Jan De Fuca where the winds are famous for blowing strong. Again it was winter and a blustery day, and as the wind blew strong she raised her arms again feeling the energy, the grandeur of it. She had never felt greater energy from the wind as she did that day.

The sound of someone approaching and then a sweet voice broke her out of her thought.

"Oh, I'm sorry, I didn't mean to startle you."

Angela looked up to see the face of a girl from her school that she recognized but didn't know.

"It's no problem, I'm Angela."

"I'm Emily. I don't want to interrupt you."

Angela just smiled, sensing she had more to say.

"I see you go up here and sit every morning and was wondering what you do?" She said looking a little embarrassed, then laughing nervously. "I mean if that's okay to ask?"

"Sure," Angela answered, "I come up here to get aligned to start the day."

"Aligned?"

"Yeah," Angela said, "One with the world around me and at peace personally."

"Wow, cool, what do you do to do that?" She hesitated, "If that's okay?"

"Sure, I become conscious of what's around me, I look, I listen, it communicates back in its' own way."

"How?"

"Here," Angela said, She gestured with her hand. "Sit down."

Emily sat down alongside Angela, facing the same way.

"Look around." Angela said and then sat quietly for minute.

"Take it all in." Then she added, "Consciously, intentionally."

She waited. Then Angela added. "Do you notice more than you did before?"

"Yes," Emily said and smiled, and laughed a little nervously again. "What do you mean communicates back?"

"It's not a conscious thing it does, it always does we just don't notice. Close your eyes." Angela closed hers as well. They sat that way for a few minutes.

"What do you hear?"

"A lot," Emily said smiling, her nervousness gone from her voice.

Angela sat quietly, her eyes still closed, waiting for Emily.

"I hear the birds. Their song is beautiful." She paused, turning her head a bit. "There are so many. They sound so busy. And, I hear them flying. I hear the wind. I hear students in the distance. Its sounds like the start of a day." She laughed happily.

Angela smiled. "That's great." Angela paused looking straight ahead. Then smiled. "This day will be different for you already."

"Feels like it," Emily said. They both sat for a few minutes, feeling the peace of the moment.

"What else do you do here?" Emily asked curiously.

"I meditate, I think about what I want to accomplish with my day, with my life. And, I keep myself aligned."

"Aligned. I want to know more about what that means."

"It's like keeping your center, your balance with you and your world. Being at peace. Alignment is when you are on the path of peace and harmony. We are prone to lose it, have to get it back."

"How?"

"Through practices every day."

"Like this." Emily added.

"Yes," Angela said with a smile, "One of them is meditation," This will make you aware of your states, how you are feeling. It's a way to prevent letting yourself be so distracted that you don't realize what's going on inside you. So like what we did so far, we first become aware of what's around us, and appreciating it, and being one with it, and then through meditation we are aware of what's happening inside of us, and react to that to keep us where we need to be. This is a process of recognizing thoughts and feelings, and replacing them when needed."

"Can you teach me to do this?" Emily asked. After a short pause she added, "I would really like to learn." She looked down then smiled, "I want what you have."

"What's that? Angela asked."

"You're different. You have a...peace about you. You seem really happy." Emily seemed to be searching hard for the words, and seemed to feel a little sad saying them. "And, you...seem...happy with who you are."

Angela smiled a tight, sweet smile at Emily. "Sure, I will, sure."

"We've talked about how to listen and look intentionally. Noticing what's around us. This will makes us more at peace in ourselves, so then we will go out into the world and spread this peace to others. Also, with how we listen and watch our environment not only gives us inner peace but makes us appreciate and have peace with it. Then, when we go out into our world we interact peacefully and don't destroy it. If we destroy our environment you can see now how that will destroy us."

"Wow," Emily said, "That is heavy man, and I like it. How do you meditate and I'm curious about more of what it does."

"Well," Angela started, "Again it's being aware of your inner state, your feelings, and not letting them control you. And, learning to not just react and have our feelings lead us, but have us be aware of them and go where we want to go, which is a path of harmony and peace. Certain feelings will prevent that."

"Like which ones?" Emily asked thoughtfully.

"Like negative, destructive thoughts." Angela said.

"How do you meditate? I always wanted to know."

"Well first you sit up, nice and straight, your back comfortably arched, looking straight ahead. Close your eyes. Recognize your thoughts as they come. Then, as you recognize them, let them go. Don't worry about analyzing them at this point. This will make you more aware of your feelings. I think you'll be surprised how many of your thoughts are negative. And when you are done you will feel relaxed, at peace."

"How long do you do this?" Emily asked.

"As long as you want. At first, two minutes will probably seem like a long time. Work up to whatever you want. This will also train your mind to not be immediately led away by your thoughts and feelings. There is an awareness, a consciousness of your feelings, then you can decide how you want to act on them, not simply be led mindlessly away by them."

"It's like those amoebas we have been working with in Biology lab. We give 'em a stimulus and they just react, nothing intermediate, nothing in between." Emily added.

"Ha, that's good, I like that. Don't be an amoeba, meditate" Angela said.

They both laughed.

Angela went on. "And then during the day do the same thing. As thoughts or feelings come, be aware of them. Meditation will make you more prone to do so automatically. Like, you'll think of something negative, or someone makes you upset, you recognize your new feeling state, and let it go, just like you did in full meditation, the practice of mediation will make this natural in you. Then, you replace that thought with a better one. That's a conscious choice."

"So you're not like an amoeba," Emily added leaning toward her, pushing Angela on the shoulder a little.

Angela laughed.

Emily looked thoughtful again. "What thoughts do you replace the negative ones with?"

"Good question. Positive thoughts. Thoughts that are in line with peace and love, not contention and selfishness. They are constructive, not destructive. These kind of thoughts also are about positive change for our lives, and that such change is possible. Our goal in life is to grow, to change in a positive direction, reach our total potential, embodying and living out these qualities."

"Wow," Emily said with a long breath. "I love it. Want to learn more."

Angela went on. "I know my major replacements for negative thoughts are things like;

'Life is about peace and harmony,'

'I am in control of my feelings, they don't control me.'

'How I feel is my choice, and I choose to be at peace, I choose joy.'

'I control whether I am joyful or not, it's my choice.'

'I'm a person of peace not contention, (like when something makes me mad).'

Or things like, 'I'm capable of doing this,' or, 'I know I can do this.'

And again, reminding yourself of something you did achieve in the past, or a task you did complete, and reminding yourself now, to help you accomplish something you want to achieve that you are too frightened to do.

Reflect and talk to yourself about your abilities, your gifts, things you know you do well, and we all have them, and how they will enable you now to reach your goal. You will feel more confident because you know that you have the tools, what it takes, to do what you want to do. Have your goal match your gifts and you will be successful. So choose something for your goal that matches what you're best at.

Tell yourself, remind yourself, as many times as you have to, especially when you are anxious or afraid.

Talk to yourself about ways you can complete the task you want to complete, the steps you will take, not letting fear take hold of you.

Replace fearful thoughts with thoughts like these, before they take over and become you.

Sometimes when a negative thought comes, such as a fearful thought, I sometimes just say to myself, 'Stop,' or Shhh, not letting it enter into my consciousness. Not letting it become me."

"One of my other favorite things is to say, 'I'm not going to enter into that world,' like when you feel something someone says or a situation is pulling you down a path you know you don't want to go. Again, that path you don't want to take is one that involves anything that is not *aligned* with the goal of peace, love and harmony.

And, if you do this long enough, you will see the changes in you, and in your life. It works."

Angela looked at Emily. Emily nodded, smiling, "Go, Go,…more."

"Also, surround yourself with positive people who will tell you good thoughts to repeat. Also, a good thing to repeat to yourself are stories of how people overcame challenges in their lives, you can remind yourself of those as well. Again, it has to be a constant practice because we are naturally prone to focus on the negative, and we will slip back to it if we stop the practice."

"Wow, thanks." Emily said. "I would really like to do this more with you, if that is cool with you?"

"I'd like that too," Angela said.

Then she added, "Oh, I want to mention one quick and easy thing you can do during the day to gain peace."

"Yeah, cool. What is it?"

"Ten deep breaths. Or as many as you have time for," Angela said smiling.

"Do it like this." Emily followed Angela's movements as they sat side by side. "Sit up tall, like when you meditate. Breathe in slowly, through your nose, your stomach moving out as you do it, and fill your chest up at the end of the breath, feel it expand as you do it. Fill up as much as you can, then slowly let it go, slowly deflating, through your mouth this time, your stomach moving back in."

They both did it together, several times.

"After you do that, you will feel different, I guarantee it, won't be feeling all stressed."

"Thanks," Emily said, really appreciate it.

The first school bell rang. They both looked up.

"Time to go," Emily said. Angela rose and grabbed her backpack. They started down the hill toward the school, Emily slightly ahead.

"Hey," Angela called gently. Emily turned. "From meeting you I'd say you have lots of reasons to like who you are for sure."

Emily smiled, "Thanks." They walked together to the school.

Right before they went their separate directions, Angela called out to Emily, "Same time tomorrow?"

Emily beamed. "Yes, great."

Ethan's mom called out to him to get ready for school. They had decided to have him transfer high schools due to the fact that he was not crazy about the quality of the teaching and heard the school on the other side of town was better. He didn't mind the extra drive but his mom knew he probably wouldn't get up early enough and might be late.

"Wake up, you have to leave earlier to get to the new school. It's going to take you longer to get there."

His mom kept after him until he answered her. Then, Ethan rolled out of bed and laid on the floor for a while. He was up late the night before reading a philosophical book that he just started that wound up being one he didn't want to stop reading, and ended up going to bed at 3:00 a.m. Good thing his mother called out to him again from downstairs, he might have slept there for hours.

He was also hoping that there would be some kids at this school who were more like him. The school he was at was very big on sports and the jocks weren't interested in anything Ethan was. He heard that the other school had kids that were into more of the things he was, the peace movement, trying to make a change in the world, making a difference. At his school he was called a freak by some kids because he had long hair and wore more psychedelic looking clothes, and wasn't into what they were into.

Ethan pulled into the parking lot of his new school, found a space to park in and then hesitated. He watched as the other kids were walking up to the school and thought to himself, "Man, I hate being the new kid." He waited a little longer, then knowing he had to go, got out of his car, threw his backpack over his shoulder and walked up to the school.

As he watched the kids milling around in the main hall he noticed more kids were dressed like him, he didn't stand out as much as he feared he would. But as the kids were all quickly hurrying around heading to class a girl grabbed his attention as she was passing through the hall. She had long blonde hair that shone bright as she passed the glass wall that leads to the courtyard outside, and had on bright colored bell bottom pants with a huge flower pattern on them and a bright colored long sleeved top with flared cuffs. She moved with an ease, a joy that made her stand out from everyone else. It was as though everyone was wearing gray and white and she alone bright colors.

He bumped into someone because he wasn't looking were he was going and when he turned around, she was gone, lost in the crowd of people. He had never seen anyone like her. He was hoping to see her again, and hoping that she would be in one of his classes. His first period class was a disappointment though, she wasn't in it.

Angela and her friend were walking into class the following period talking and sat down together still in their conversation. They're conversation ended when Ethan walked in the room.

"Whoa, who's that?" Her friend whispered.

"Never seen him before," Angela answered. "But I like the way he dresses. Very cool."

Ethan walked down the main row of chairs and smiled a quick sweet smile at Angela and sat down. Angela's friend smiled at her and nudged her with her elbow. When class started the teacher had Ethan stand up and introduce himself to the class. She had him tell his name and what interests he had. He mentioned he loved philosophy and trying to make a difference in the world. The teacher said that she was impressed and welcomed him to the school. Angela's friend nudged her again.

The next morning Angela and Emily met before school and sat and listened and mediated. Emily had picked it all up quickly and it made it a really good time for both of them. At the end Emily asked if she could have a friend of hers come and Angela said sure. The group grew as word spread how great the time with Angela was and how much people were benefiting from her teaching. Soon there were over a dozen girls meeting every morning and listening to everything Angela was teaching them.

The group kept growing steadily over the next few months, more kids coming every week.

The group all met in the middle of tall trees at the top of the hill before school as they usually do. Everyone settled in and the beauty and peacefulness of the scene was evident affecting them all. There was a smooth breeze and the trees swayed as it went making a soft, soothing sound, the green grass was tall enough that it swayed in the breeze as well. Everyone looked calm and relaxed.

One of the girls broke the silence. "I love what you're teaching us about these things and I feel great when I'm here, and then I go on with the day and I react the same as I used to, and by the end of the day I'm all twisted up again."

"Don't be discouraged. Our natural tendency is to do just what you said, to go back to where we were. Staying at this consistently is really important, Angela answered. The longer you do this the more of a lasting deep effect it will have on you, but you have to stay at it a while before you will really see the difference. The other thing is you have to take these practices and do them all day. Just like how when we meditate we recognize our thoughts and let them go, we have to do that during the day also. When we start really paying attention to our thoughts we will definitely be amazed by how much of our thoughts are negative. So as they come into your mind, recognize them and then let them go. So then during the day, we have to do the same. Eventually, you will see how your mind does it all the time. This is a major part of the path to peace for yourself and with the world. And replace your negative thoughts with positive ones. So, you're feeling angry at something your teacher did, remind yourself that you are about peace not war, harmony not contention. Don't let yourself think thoughts you know you don't want."

One of the girls, named Shonice chimed in. "So we do what we do here, all the time."

"Yes," Angela answered enthusiastically, "If it doesn't become us its just external, like playing a game."

Another girl joined in. "Like when Johnny shot that comment at you yesterday in class, he is such a..."

"And believe me," Angela added quickly, "I had to remind myself quickly of my goal, before I entered into his world."

"And that goal is?" Emily asked.

"Being at peace with the world, and with people as much as is possible."

"He's such a jerk." Someone else added.

"I've heard he even grabbed some girl and tried to kiss her."

"If he tried that with me, he'd be 'pieces,' that's the peace he'd get," Shonice said.

"Yeah, what about that," Emily asked?

"I agree with her," Angela said.

"Right on girl!" someone called out.

"But, it was because I *had* to defend myself, but wasn't looking for it. I don't want to be at odds with the world where any little thing sets me off."

"I agree, and most of that is just some kind of macho reaction," Shonice added.

"Man, we could talk forever with all the cool stuff you guys keep bringing up, I love it." Angela said with a big grin. "Yeah, that's a great example. I'm so glad all you guys are here."

Angela continued. "Yeah, doing things, reacting, out of ego instead of out of the goal of harmony, of peace. We don't want the most important thing in our lives to be pride, most worried about what people think of us and not letting them 'mess with us' because of our ego."

"That's different than protecting your body, or life." Shonice added.

"Absolutely." Angela said. "I like a lot of the wisdom that comes from the East, we need more of it here in the West. There was a story of a Kung Fu student hundreds of years ago in China who went to his master and asked him about this same thing.

He asked, 'Master, what if someone blocks my path?'

'Take another path,' his master answered quickly.'

'What if they block that path?'

'Then contend without contending,' he told him.'"

Emily excitedly spoke up. "Cool, I got it. He's saying you do what you have to defend your life but you don't act like them."

"Yeah, and don't become them," Shonice added.

"Right." Angela said. "Your peace is maintained. You are not adding to that part of you that just wants to elevate yourself over others for your own sake. You are nourishing the part of you that you want to grow, and let the other part wither away."

"So, if you act like Johnny, you become more like him. You'll become like that sad soul." Shonice added. Laughs were heard in the group.

Angela laughed. "You're not only smart, you're funny as well."

"She is," another said with a laugh.

"You always want to have in your mind your goal of peace and harmony. The more you do the more you hear it when it counts most." Angela said.

"The more we fill our minds with what we want to be, the more we will become it." Shonice added.

Emily spoke up. "So we fill our minds with our goals, like you said, and we meditate. I know we talked about this, but for everyone else, what else helps fill our minds the way we want?"

"What we read is big. What we listen to. Who we hang out with. I want my closest friends to be guys like you guys," Angela added. But I want to be around all people also as I have opportunities. I love people, and I want to influence the world." "Also," Angela added, wanting to not forget it, "What we listen to is important also, music wise."

Sharon, who has a great voice starting singing, "A time for peeeaacce, I swear it's not too late"

"They got that right," Another added.

Mary chimed in. "Tell it to me slowly, tell you what, I really want to know,"

And then all the girls harmonized together loudly, "It's the time...of the seeeeeason for loving!"

"I love our group!" Emily called out.

Angela could see the change in Emily since she joined the group. She just seemed to come alive. They had become best friends very quickly and spent a lot of their free time together. So much had happened since that day Emily walked up the hill and met Angela.

The bell rang that homeroom was about to begin in five minutes.

Everyone started heading to the school. As they were all walking back splitting into groups and going different directions, Angela was walking alone and noticed someone who had been sitting on the grass reading, gathering all of his things into his backpack to go to class. She noticed it was the new boy who just transferred to the school.

As she approached a couple of the books fell out of his backpack. Angela was behind him and bent down to pick them up for him. She stood and they were facing each other closely. They both kind of froze and looked at each other. After a pause. Angela held out her hand,

"I'm Angela, welcome to the school."

Ethan paused. "The girl who wears the bright flower pants," he thought.

"Uh, hi, I'm Ethan."

Angela smiled back. Angela forgot she had the books for a second. "Oh, here's your books, you dropped them."

"Thanks," he said.

Angela looked at the titles before she handed them to him. "Walden," by Henry David Thoreau," she looked up and smiled. Then she read the other title, "Plato's

Republic? I'm impressed. This is not the typical books most students have in their backpacks."

"Oh, I'm sure they'll think I'm the geek of the week."

"Who cares," Angela said.

They started walking together. "So these books are for a class? If they are I want to take it."

"No," Ethan said, "They're for me."

"Huh." Angela said.

They walked the rest of the way to the school without talking, but both were in deep thought about the other. Ethan broke the silence.

"Well, this is where I turn off." They looked at each other. Ethan pointed in the direction he needed to go. My class is that way."

Both seemed a little dazed.

"Oh, of course," Angela said, and they both laughed.

They both went their separate ways, no doubt occupied with dreamy thoughts about the other. Angela's ethereal moment was short as she was abruptly interrupted by Anita, an employee of the school who knew her well and also with whom she had had many lively talks with about politics.

"Angela, you are not going to believe this, they are firing Superintendent Abromovitz!"

"What! Why?"

"They are mad I know, because of his political views! I know it! They have totally been after him ever since he came out against the war. They have always wanted to get rid of him from the very beginning."

"I can't believe this." Angela said in loud whisper, looking down thinking. "When he took over, he totally turned this district around. It's a top rated district now academically. He added debate classes and clubs, encouraged the students to speak out, voice their opinions, strongly, but intelligently."

"I know, It's ridiculous! They are railroading him."

"I don't believe it"

"Believe it. The student involvement stuff made them mad but what really set them off was his being sure the school was not segregated and busing kids from neighborhoods that weren't able to come here before, that's what really did it. Now they have an excuse."

"What excuse?"

"They are saying he's being subversive to his country by coming out publicly against the war and that he is intentionally poisoning the minds of the students." Anita stiffened up and clenched her fists. "I was so bummed when I first heard, now I'm hacked!"

Angela was looking down as she does when she is deep in thought, thinking of what to do, as Anita raged on. Anita was still going on with her outrage when Angela interrupted.

"I got it!" She shook her finger up and down.

"Come with me!" She ordered Anita, and she pulled her with her and then ran them to the school office.

Over the next two days Angela met with school leaders, and asked for permission to speak with the board who were firing the superintendent. They gave her permission to go speak to the board in behalf of Abramovitz.

All of the girls from her morning meeting and several other students joined her as she went to go speak to the school board. The board was very surprised that a student wanted to come present to them especially in behalf of a school official. They were more than blown away when they heard her speak.

She opened her speech with a recap of the men and women who have made great contributions to society through diligent and thoughtful work such as our founding fathers and how they fought for justice and a way of life unlike any in the world. They were feeling bowled over as she continued to describe their sacrifice for freedom and our unparalleled system of government.

Their whole countenance changed though when she brought up Martin Luther King and Rosa Parks. Great agents of change in our own era she called them. Champions of justice, she called out. All of the faces of the board dropped. The students noticed their reaction including some who were at this school as a result of Abromovitz's program to expand the district to include more minority students. These students looked outraged at the change in demeanor of the board as Angela went on about civil rights in her presentation.

The board members started to look uncomfortable and some were seen squirming in their seats. Angela had purposely done this to try and demonstrate their injustice. That was the main reason why she wanted the press to be there, to hopefully film their reaction. The press did film the speech and the event but Angela was not sure if they captured the boards' change in demeanor. It had turned out that the press did not capture it, but so many more people from the town showed up than expected, and they noticed it. Fortunately, they were on the side of civil rights and Abromovitz's political agenda.

When Angela was finished with her speech, the crowd cheered. The board looked at each other with blank expressions and then back to the crowd. The Chairman of the school board stood up to speak. He dryly thanked Angela for her speech and then made a foolish political move by announcing without any discussion among his fellow board members their decision to fire Abromovitz. People started to get loud and the crowd began to get irate and point and shout at the board members. No one had noticed that now police officers lined the walls on the side of the hall until the Chairman of the school board gestured to the Chief of police to intervene. Angela could see where this was going and went to the microphone again.

"Good Chairman." She spoke louder. "I need everyone's attention."

Everyone began to quiet down, enough for Angela to be heard.

"Good Chairman, our esteemed school board. I assure you that police intervention will not be necessary. We advocate peace, and as the greatest men of our era and perhaps any other such as Dr. Martin Luther King advocate, peace and thoughtful action is what we are about, not violent dissention. We." Angela waved her arms to encompass every one of the students and adult community supporters. "We will leave as we came in, peacefully." She looked directly into the eyes of the Chairman. "Thank you sir for your time and attention."

And with that she walked off the podium and led everyone out of the building calmly.
They all filed out behind Angela and out into the parking lot. Angela saw Anita on the way out as they were walking out. "This is not over yet." She told her.

The next day Angela started contacting the leaders of the all of the schools in the district. They all agreed with her that this was an injustice and that he shouldn't be fired but thought nothing could be done. Angela convinced them that something really could be done and asked them to join her. She convinced the leaders of all the schools in the district to let her organize a district wide walkout.

Everything was ready. The day of the walkout came. Every school was ready and people were waiting because the plan was that Angela was going to lead her school ahead of the others and they would all walk to the center of town and then Angela and a teacher would give a speech. The school board members heard of the plan and thought the best way to stop it was to focus all of their resources on the high school Angela attended. They enlisted the help of the local police to prevent any activity to begin at the high school which would get the whole protest rolling. Stop the leader at the source was the idea.

The police began to arrive at the high school. The school board chairman knew the police presence would intimidate the students and staff and definitely end the protest. Everyone was watching the line of police cars pull up to the school, standing up and moving to the windows and pointing out and talking among themselves. Everyone was definitely intimidated. Word reached the classroom room Angela was in for homeroom. She moved to a window where she could see what was happening. She ran out of the room and up the school's office. She convinced the office staff to let her use the school's P.A. system which broadcasts throughout the school in every room.

After a whine of feedback Angela's voice was heard over the speakers.

"All teachers, staff, and students. In times like this we all need to remember why we are doing what we are doing and not be moved by people trying to intimidate and scare us away from doing what is right. We stand on the foundation of the solid promises of what makes this country great. To borrow a great phrase from a great man, we will not be moved. What we need now is courage and conviction. We need to take action but we need to do it together, then we will prevail. Our freedom and the freedom of future students who will sit in the same chairs that we sit in now is at stake. Everyone meet me at the great hill in the back of school. Love you all."

Music began to play after Angela finished. It was the band, The Who singing, "Let's see action." The music played over the speakers and students rose and began filing out of the doors toward the back of the school. The beat of the song fit the cadence of everyone resolutely filing out. The song strongly called for action, not allowing people to be passive, seeing freedom as the goal.

In the classroom Ethan sat in, the students were filing out of the door. Ethan smiled a proud smile and shook his head approvingly. "Incredible," he said. And he followed the other students out the door and toward the great hill at the back of the school as the song continued to play filling the students with conviction and enthusiasm, driving them forward, past their fears; the strong lyrics and the driving beat, the call for action, the stakes, their freedom.

Students and staff were pouring out of the back if the building, walking calmly but resolutely, stoutly determined now, energy in their steps, led by their leader standing at the top of the hill. The speakers for the school that broadcast Angela's message and now the song could be heard outside the school, resounding beautifully, keeping time with the energized crowd who were making history that day.

Students and teachers were filling the great grass hill behind the school while Angela waited on top. Ethan looked up smiling at the wonderful young lady he had just had the pleasure of meeting and wanted to know so much more about. She was everything he'd dreamed all his life about. As the last students filed out, the song continued to play, encouraging everyone to stand strong.

The music ended. The crowd was strangely silent. Angela called loudly from the top of the hill to the huge crowd swarming the area with no bit of grass on the ground to be seen, paraphrasing the song just heard. "I do see people, I do see action, let's be free, let's show we care!" And with that she began down the side of the hill to leave the school grounds and meet up with the other schools in the walkout.

The Chairman of the school board told the police to make a human barricade to prevent the crowd from leaving the school. Mr. Wallace, an English teacher at the school anticipated this and was right there and asked the news team he invited to stand with him. He knew that would be critical to stop the Chairman's plan. He spoke directly to Captain of the police.

"This is their right. They are peaceful, they are thoughtful, no hint of malice or violence. Are you going to stand between them and their right to do this, and in public view and on television for all to see?" The police Captain said nothing after he spoke. Then he stood back, the television cameras continually rolling.

The students left the school grounds and met up with the other schools in a smooth, fluid line. The path they chose allowed them to pick up each school to join them, adding to their number greatly as they went forward toward the town square. The scene was incredible. The will of the people in action.

The huge throng met quietly but powerfully in the town square. Angela and Mr. Wallace spoke eloquently and with conviction, and without any incident at all. The event was on the local and national news. Superintendent Abromovitz was reinstated to his job. Shortly after, due to public pressure, the Chairman of the school board resigned.

At the end of the day, Angela knew she needed to be alone. She retreated to the hill where she met with her group every morning before school. She sat and allowed her mind to process the day. At first her mind was loud despite the cool and quiet scene where she sat. She sat on her blanket on top of soft green grass. Tall trees created a canopy only allowing glowing streaks of sunlight in, diffuse and warm. But the day was so frenetic and loud that her mind was still loud. She just sat. She worked on her breathing without any thoughts. She allowed her mind to work through all that happened and eventually she knew the sounds of the day would work their way through and all that would be left at the end would be silence inside her, and the sounds of the outside around her; the birds, the wind, and she would be centered again, in harmony.

She knew also that she wasn't supposed to just sit, to just contemplate. She knew that she needed to use her gifts, as we all have, in our own unique way, for the good of others and to facilitate that what she has attained inside, to the world around her outside. She dreamed of the harmony she worked for on a daily basis to spread to the whole world. She sat for a while longer, then finally felt calm. The timing was perfect for what happened next.

She heard someone coming up from the wooded area behind. It was Ethan. He smiled.

"Hey." He said.

"Hey," she answered back.

"Is it okay if I join you? Don't want to ruin your peace."
"You won't ruin my peace, believe me."

He sat beside her on the blanket. "That was incredible today."

"I'm just so grateful for all the support," Angela said, "and that it went so well. A good man kept his job thanks to the people."

Ethan smiled and looked ahead. He loved how she didn't mention herself, nor wanted to. "I was inspired by you today. I think you are a really great person and I really want to get to know you better." He turned to her and smiled. "How do you feel about that?"

She smiled back. "I'd like that very much." Angela looked straight ahead and then back to Ethan. "You can start by reading some of that Thoreau to me."

"That sounds great," he said. "I happen to have it right here." Ethan took the book out of backpack and started reading.

"Most of the luxuries, and many of the so-called comforts of life, are not only not indispensable, but positive hindrances to elevation of mankind. With respect to luxuries and comforts, the wisest have ever lived a simple and meager life than the poor. The ancient philosophers, Chinese, Hindu, Persian, and Greek, were a class than which none have been poorer."

"Speak it," she said.

He smiled and went on. He looked a little further down the page, found the spot with his finger and went on.

"There are nowadays professors of philosophy, but not philosophers. Yet it is admirable to profess because it was once admirable to live. To be a philosopher is not merely to have subtle thoughts, nor even to found a school, but so to love wisdom as to live according to its dictates, a life of simplicity, independence, magnanimity, and trust.

It is to solve some of the problems of life, not only theoretically but practically."

Ethan stopped reading and looked up. He turned and smiled at Angela. "That's what happened today."

She smiled dropping her head a bit.

5

Love of a Brother

The group met as it did each week, several months going by and they all grew closer. One week they had some surprise guests join the morning group. Clair, a woman who worked in the office and Janet an English teacher at the school both joined. The two women walked up just as it was about to start. Everyone was already sitting and they weren't sure what to expect as they approached the group.

Janet spoke first. "Hi." She looked at everyone. "Good morning. We heard you were leading a group in the mornings before school and that you let new people in." She stopped and looked at everyone again smiling. The kids, surprised, just looked at her.

Angela broke the silence. "Sure." And she gestured for them to sit down. "You're both totally welcome." "I think it's very cool you want to be part of our scene."

"Groovy." Emily said.

"Surprised though." Shonice said with a smile. Everyone laughed.

"The timing is really cool," Angela said because I wanted to talk about what happens to adults when they get out of high school or college and go to work."

"The rat race," Janet said aptly.

"Perfect metaphor," Angela said.

"And there are plenty of rats. I tell you girl." Shonice added. The group laughed.

Angela opened up the conversation. "It makes me sad thinking of kids graduating, and where their heads were full of dreams, then they lose that as they get older." The kids were nodding, heads gesturing in agreement. Their eyes were fixed on Angela. "We can't let situations govern our lives. People often have their happiness be determined by their circumstances, by what happens to them. Things will happen in our lives, positive and negative. How we view them is huge. We have to embrace what is but look for the positive aspect or result that can come. I think people let circumstances in life beat them down and this is part of what destroys their "dream state" as I like to call it. We need to see these tough times as "fuel" to be motivated to change our lives, we can't let them ruin us. Sometimes these things are even necessary to get us going. For instance, you may hate your job and that should motivate or "fuel" you as I said to make a change, to get out. And also looking for the positives in each situation, you may realize when you look around and see how other people are treated at work, that you don't have it as bad as you thought you did.

Another important thing is to learn to flow with what comes your way, embrace it, feel it, but keep your positive outlook, let nothing destroy that. Never let anything take away your childlike enthusiasm and wonder for the world, and your dreams as you had when you were a child. Keep dreaming, keep making it happen."

Shonice let out a breath, "Heavy." Then she added. "So do we do this the same way we do with maintaining personal peace?"

"Yes," Angela answered, "It all comes from practice, from what you put into your mind. You read books that grow you in this direction. You can learn to stop thoughts that are contrary like we talked about before with meditation, and self-talk. And remember, how we react to things that happen to us in our lives is our choice."

"Self-talk?" Sharon who was new to the group asked.

"I have conversations with myself." Angela said. "I talk these things through in my mind. I remind myself of what I believe. I talk myself away from fear and from letting it rule me."

"Cool," Janet said, leaning forward. "What kinds of things do you say?"

"And I also have to say first that this self-talk flows from the practice of meditation. You learn to be conscious of your thoughts, to be aware of them as they come, and then you don't just act immediately on your feelings or emotions as they come to you, like an amoeba being prodded like we did in Biology lab, remember that?" She said laughing a bit. "And I thank Emily for that analogy, she used it as an example one time when we were talking about this. That's what we're like when we just react to everything without any control. So now, because of your practice of meditation, you would be aware of the change in your emotional state and then be able to do the self-talk we are talking about.

So, for example, let's say someone had done something that irritated me, and I feel this reaction welling up in me," Angela smiled and sat up taller, and raised her arms like a big bear about to snatch its prey. "And then I told myself, your goal is peace."

People were chuckling from her display. Angela had to laugh for a second. "And then I said again, You're about peace with the world. And at that moment after I was aware of my feeling state, because I have trained myself to be aware in meditation, I was able to catch it and not let it rule and reign me, and then replace it with something better. And not be an Amoeba".

With that you could hear laughter among the group. "And," Angela continued, "I felt at peace. I let it go and felt at peace. And, sometimes, I can tell you, it takes more than a couple of words to feel that peace."

Sharon added. "Sometimes it takes more than a couple of times, you're not kidding. I mean it could be something serious and you just want to…and ummmm." And she made a fist and tightened her jaw.

That caused chuckles in the group and expressions of agreement mingled throughout.

"Yes, if it's major it won't be that fast, then keep doing what we do, don't stay focused on it. Keep working to ge your center back, your harmony. Don't just let your feelings run you away, or astray."

"That's better than saying, 'not letting your feelings run away with you.' I got it and agree", Shonice added.

Angela went on. "The more you do this, the faster you will feel yourself change, and get back to where you want to be. Also, when I may feel fear for instance about something I want to do or something I am afraid of, I remind myself of who I know myself to be, of the abilities given me, and also of how badly I want that certain goal, and of how much my attitude will affect the outcome. I read a lot of positive quotes from people. I also read stories of perseverance and recall them when I need to be reminded; that also keeps me in perspective. I see what other people have overcome, and usually it's more than I have to deal with. I also think of things I can do, actions I can take to improve my situation, and that gives me hope and confidence as well. I also pray for the strength to do what I know I need to, and thanks for what I was able to do."

Emily added, "You also said once that people who have a negative filter or tend to think in a negative sense, tend to remember only the bad things and forget the good things. Their memories have better recall of negative things than positive things."

"Yes, and it shows how powerful our thoughts can be. Remember the positive." Janet said.

Shawn, a guy who recently joined the group, added, "Also the people we hang out with. Negative people, can be a real drag, bring you down."

Emily nodded "That's right. Your closest friends have to be positive." She looked around the group. "Like you guys."

Angela jumped in and added. "I totally agree Em, and we can try to help those though who aren't, who live with a negative filter, seeing everything from a negative perspective, always seeing why something can't be done, not happy no matter what comes their way. It may be too much to have them really close but our goal is to show them a better way."

Shonice jumped in. "And that helps me not get mad at them also, because I feel bad that they live that way and want to help them see the light, hallelujah!" saying the last part with emphasis, drawing laughter around the group. The group was laughing and talking, reacting to what Shonice said. After a couple of minutes Angela waved her hands a bit.

"I just wanted to add one more thing before the bell rings, about this. Not losing your joy, and especially as we go further in our lives, will be determined by us. By how we react to things, how we manage our thoughts. With a positive perspective everything changes, we see the world in a totally different light. It all becomes about possibilities. We can turn things around in our lives but there has to be that positive foundation driving it. You build a house on a solid foundation, not a weak one, it won't hold anything up. Remember these things, carry them with you. Develop these habits. Never let anything or anyone try to rob you of your joy. It's all your choice. You always will have the power to keep it."

"Go girl, go," Shonice said encouragingly.

Angela smiled at her friend, "People will say to you, 'How are you always happy, you always seem so joyful, full of life.' How?" She looked at everyone in the group. "Doing all of techniques we talked about, meditation, appreciation/unity with the world around us, positive self-talk, reading inspirational and philosophical books that will grow us and expand our minds, and will increase our fascination and wonder about life and why we are here, instead of just going after money or prestige, thinking that will make us happy. Those things don't bring total fulfillment and true lasting joy. So keep that positive foundation for how you interact with the world. And that comes from appreciating the little things, finding the joy in them instead of totally missing it. Being blown away by what we have instead of focusing on what we don't have."

"That's huge," Janet added.

Angela nodded and smiled at her. "Think of a child. Remember, our goal is to retain and grow the childlike wonder and enthusiasm in us. What is the child like? They are so appreciative of the little things. They get so excited by them. They find such joy in them; watching the clouds and figuring out the shapes, running outside excitedly when it rains, dancing and stomping in the puddles, watching a butterfly. They also get so excited about getting to spend a small amount of true quality time with someone they love. Do we do that with the ones we love? Just appreciating them and being excited about just spending some quality time together, instead of it always having to be some big event to have any meaning?"

Angela stopped and smiled at the group, looking at all of them. "You all have the potential for this in you, for the kind of joy and peace and harmony we have been talking about here every day. You all have your own unique gifts to cultivate and grow and then give to the world. Don't let it fall short, don't allow anyone to rob you of the life you were meant to live. And don't deprive the world of what you can do for it with your gifts."

The bell rang.

"I love you guys."

Someone was heard giving a disappointed, "Ahh." But it was time to go.

As they were all getting up Janet came up to Angela. "Thanks for letting me come, that was amazing, I really enjoyed it. And, we should hang out some time."

"I'd like that," Angela said. And they walked back together to the school.

After school Angela stopped at Emily's house to hang out. No one seemed to be home. She knocked and no one answered. She tried the door and it opened. No one seemed to be there, so she started out, closing the door behind her when she heard crying. She reopened the door. "Emily?" She called out. There was no answer, so Angela started up the stairs to Emily's room. She slowly opened the door and Emily was on the edge of her bed crying. One of her hands was holding her head and the other was holding a letter.

"What's happening kiddo?" Angela said softly.

Emily was saying something but Angela couldn't understand through her tears. "What, what's up, couldn't hear you," Angela said softly, sitting down beside her.

"This." Emily handed Angela a letter. It was a draft notice. Angela felt her heart sink. For a second she couldn't breathe. Emily's brother had been called to serve in Vietnam, leaving right away. Angela sat in stunned silence. Emily was crying as Angela stared out the window trying to take it all in and compose herself so she could help her friend. She gave Emily a hug. Emily began to cry harder.

Angela held her there for a long time until Emily sat up, her face red, tears running down. "No, no, no, they can't have him, they can't take Brian." Emily started to panic. Her crying became hysterical, she began hyperventilating.

Angela grabbed her shoulders and looked right in her eyes. "Emily, Emily. Look at me."

Emily calmed down a little but wouldn't look at Angela.

"Em, it's me, Ange. Look at me."

Emily looked up, her face covered in tears and beet red.

"It's me, it's Ange, listen to me."

Emily looked down again.

"Look at me. You are not in this alone, you are not in this alone. Whatever happens in our lives we go through together."

Emily stopped crying, she lost her breath a couple of times but was calming down. Angela still held her firmly. "Together." She was still looking right in her eyes. Angela smiled and turned her head as she said it again for emphasis and gave Emily's a little shake. "Together."

Angela waited as Emily continued to calm down.

"Okay?"

Emily smiled and spoke in a small voice, "Okay."

She helped Emily stand up. "Where is everybody?"

"I have no idea where Brian is. Probably with his friends. My folks are at my uncle's, freaking out. Everybody's freaking out.

"Well, you're coming with me," Angela said.

"Where?"

"To my house. You are not going to be alone. I'm going to help get all your stuff, you're sleeping over."

Angela helped Emily pack everything she needed and they walked over to her house. Angela's mother gave her lots of hugs and comforted her as much as she could considering what was happening. Emily had always been extremely close to her older brother, and this meant much more to her because she didn't really have the greatest relationship with her father. He was gone most of the time traveling on business and when he was home was not really interested in her, but Brian was another story. Her father was crazy about his son.

Emily and her mother weren't close either. Her mother used to be full of life and happy very much like the way Emily is now but the marriage to her father seemed to change that. He became aloof towards her and overbearing when it came to any kind of decision around the house. He was domineering and not very loving, thinking a woman's place was in the kitchen and to keep her mouth shut. Emily says that he sucked the life right out of her. She thinks her mother resents her for reminding her of what she used to be when she was young and full of dreams. She thinks her mom sees in her what was in her past and what is not for her now. She knows her mother is miserable and withdrawn and this wears on Emily terribly. She feels sad for her mother and hurt at the same time.

It was much better for Emily to be over at Angela's house. Angela felt so badly for her she told her mother when they were alone, and that she wishes she could always stay with them and never have to go home. Her mother told her that you never know what the future will hold with her and her family but wanted to take away Emily's pain also.

The day came shortly after for Brian to leave and head oversees. Angela knew this was going to be awful and couldn't imagine what her friend was feeling.

Angela went with Emily to where the buses were going to drive the recruits to the base and then they would be eventually shipped out for service. There was a lot of commotion and soldiers in uniform milling around and families crying everywhere Angela could see. Cars were pulling in and out and parking all around as many families were dropping their sons off.

Some protesters had set up a booth outside the base on the street and were playing antiwar songs and shouting over a loud speaker. Angela agreed with protesting against the war but to do this here as they were was just making it so much worse for the soldiers and their families.

Brian was ready to board his bus as the music played loudly over the speakers. This did not help the situation, Angela felt terribly for Emily.

Angela always loved these groups, but not here, not today. The music blared over the speakers as Brian and the others boarded the bus. It added to the grief of the moment.

The bus started to pull away. Emily started to run after it. Angela ran with her, and she could hear the music playing the song as they ran, and Brian waving as the bus pulled further and further away. His arm that was out of the window getting smaller and smaller.

Angela had Emily stay with them for a while. She did not want her to go home and be reminded of her brother everywhere she went. She needed support, she needed love. The tragic part of it, that Emily could not escape was that she never heard from her parents at all during that three week period. They knew where to contact her if they wanted to, but never did. Angela felt so deeply for her friend in such pain. Emily was such a sweet spirit, full of life, love and joy, and Angela was going to do all she could that it stayed that way all of her days.

6

Empower not Empire

Monday was the next time the group met. And when Angela arrived there were a lot more kids than in the usual group. Word had continued to spread about the group and how much people were influenced by it and really enjoying the teaching. Janet mentions it in her English classes when the subject calls for it and that helped add to the number. The protest also made a huge difference, so many people blown away by what they saw from her. It troubled Angela though to see so many people waiting for the meeting. In an instant the size of the crowd changed the topic for today. She felt she had to use the increase in the group as an opportunity, instead of a potentially very negative situation, with people being too enamored with her and following her like a cult leader. This created the situation, and created the opportunity to empower the people against being drawn into a cult by an unscrupulous leader.

"Hi guys," Angela said as she sat down with everyone. "Wow, big group today. This gave me the thought to talk about something different today with you guys. You have heard in the news about various cult groups that have popped up and create disturbing headlines about people leaving their homes or slavishly obeying a leader and all that. What leaders should do is empower people, equip people, not build a personal following, and not use people to suit their own purposes like for money or power or whatever else. Beware of this. Beware of someone who wants your total allegiance and exerts strong pressure to stay. Beware of groups where the meetings drag on and they deprive you of a chance to rest or get food. This is done sometimes purposely to be able to gain power over you. When people are tired and hungry it easier to do.

But sometimes it won't be like that. Unhealthy groups a not always so overt. Many times it is much more subtle but you will still feel the pressure. Maybe it would be feeling the social pressure to come out with a confessior or pressure to put them before your friends and family and try to pull you away from them.

Don't be fooled. It has to be about love above all else, and love doesn't do any of that. It should be about empowering you, and equipping you. This is no following the guru. You want teachers, yes. You want mentors, yes. But their job is to enrich you and build yo up so you can model it for others, and so that you can teach others yourself and pass it on and on. Don't be fooled. Remember, it can be subtle but powerful. Sound good?"

The wind picked up and swept smoothly but powerfully through the group. The trees swayed high at the top as i went.

"There we go," Angela said. "There's our answer."

Everyone laughed.

They got into a discussion about it, and went over the different points Angela brought up, many people sharin their experiences and opinions on it.

"I wanted to bring something else up real quick for you guys," Angela said, changing the subject. "It's somethir I do everyday and I want to be sure to share it with you. You know we have been talking a lot about meditation and how sometimes we sit and do it for long periods in silence, in seclusion, and how we also do it during our day as thoughts come into our minds. Well, also I do a brief form of it, especially when I'm having a really busy day. I'll do what I call short meditations or alignments. Sometimes I think of them as quick appreciations because it always involves nature and admiring it. What I'll do is when I have a short break in a very busy day, or any day for that matter, I'll stop for a minute or so, and focus on some aspect of the environment around me. I'll stop and look a tree, or maybe step out of my house when I've been studying for a while in my room and just look at the garden, or into the yard.

I'll be quiet and listen, look and admire, and calm and align my spirit as it should be. I do this all the time during a typical day. Don't substitute this though for longer periods of meditation, but add this into your day as a matter of practice. It helps you keep your perspective on what is really important. This can also be thought of as one of the 'little things' we talked about, when we were talking about kids and being joyful and loving the little things and not always waiting for big happy events to come along, or depending on them for joy.

Life is more in the little things. Try this. And it can be as simple as looking up at a tree or the sky before stepping into a building for an appointment you have. Even for a few seconds, you stop, look, focus completely, intentionally, so that nothing is in your mind at all. Smile and take it in, feel the air, the breeze. Take in the beauty of something simple, let it enter in. Then, go back on your way. The difference in how you feel will be amazing.

One last thing related to it is quick breathing exercises. I always advocate doing breathing exercises to have harmony and health physically, and I know I've gone over how to do proper breathing exercises before, a bunch of times. But here I'm talking about doing it when your time is limited. It is a very powerful tool. It is done the same way as the traditional breathing exercise but just shorter. So, wherever you are in your day, and especially when you are feeling stressed or upset in some way, do a short breathing exercise. Inhale slowly through your nose, your stomach expanding out as you go. Take the fullest breath you can, fill your entire chest cavity. Then, exhale slowly, through your mouth, your stomach deflating. Ideally ten is usually the number I like people to do but when you don't have enough time do as many as you do have time for. You will really feel the difference after, physically and mentally. It's great."

The group practiced the breathing for the remainder of their time together.

The next day a young sophomore named Amy stopped Angela before lunch and asked if she could talk to her. She said yes. The girl backed up to a space between the row of lockers and the doorway of an empty classroom so no one would hopefully hear her.

"I need your advice. I was dating this guy," She paused, looked around, seeming embarrassed. "He, broke up with me." She kept looking down, and was trying to not cry.

"And then, he came up to me today and said, that he wanted to get back together again."

"I'm sorry," Angela said, "If I can ask, did he tell you why he wanted to break up with you?"

"He just said that he didn't want to go out with me anymore."

"What did you say to him when he said he wanted to go out with you again?"

"I told him I don't know."

"Then what did he say to you?"

"He said, let him know."

"And then he walked away?"

"Yes."

Angela thought for a second, then said, "Let's go have lunch." Angela took Amy across the street to a deli in an office building next to the school.

She sat them down at a table away from everyone. She ordered food for them and sat down with her. "So tell me. What do think of all this?"

"What do you mean?" Amy asked?

"Well, what do you think of the whole conversation, how it went down. I mean, you were going out, and then he said he wanted to break up with you, and now he's saying he wants to get back together. I'm just wondering what you think of how he treated you, what do you think of that?"

"I didn't like it."

"So what are you thinking of doing now?"

"I don't know", she said.

Angela breathed out a long breath. She felt so bad for this girl. And wanted her to answer back that she was disgusted by how he treated her and she was going to tell him to take a hike. She felt disappointed but didn't want to show it. But Amy was not really responding, and didn't seem to be getting it, so Angela finally decided she had to spell it out more directly.

"I have to say, it was not cool the way he treated you. He broke up with you and didn't even tell you why. He then came back and said that he wanted to get back together, and again didn't say anything about why, and then when you said you didn't know, he just said to let him know. And through the whole thing it seemed he wasn't very nice to you about it either, huh?"

"No."

"So what do you think that says to you?"

Amy hesitated, looked down and off to the distance a couple of times and then looked at Angela.

"That he's a jerk and I shouldn't go out with him."

"Yes!" Angela slapped her hand hard on the table. Everyone in the deli looked over. She didn't seem to care in the least. She was just so happy at the young girl's answer.

"Okay, so what are you going to tell this guy?"

"I'm going to tell him that I don't want to go out with him anymore?"

"Why are you phrasing it as a question?"

"I don't know."

"Amy, you are worth more than that. You deserve to be treated as you should be. He was cold and insensitive to you. Is that honestly what you want for yourself?"

"No." She hesitated, bit her lip a bit, and added, "But I don't like being alone either."

"Nothing is worth that. I'd choose to be alone for a thousand years than be with someone like that for one minute. You are a valuable person. You're precious. Don't put up with that from anyone. And it's important to be able to be alone and be fine. You never want to go out with someone because you don't want to be alone. You may think you're solving something for yourself at the moment, but you will be in for nothing but pain later being with someone like that. You should be with someone who adores you and cares for you because of who you are."

Angela felt frustrated because she didn't think she was getting anywhere with Amy. It seemed to Angela that she was going to get back together with "that guy." How could she convince her of her value? How could she convince her also that you have to be ok with being alone and not go out with someone because you can't stand being alone? She went on to tell Amy these things anyway even though she was getting the impression that Amy made up her mind to get back together with him. Angela was saddened by the fact that she knew Amy was going to have to learn the hard way by living it out and didn't want her to through that pain, and she absolutely hated seeing this young girl being treated like that by anyone. She felt powerless and frustrated as she walked back with Amy to the school.

The bell rang when they got up to the school. Angela suddenly had a thought about a way to help Amy.

"Hey, why don't you come to our morning group before school every day? Be fun to hang out. What do you say?"

Amy looked surprised. "You want me to come?" But it's almost all Seniors?"

Angela smiled at Amy. "Of course I want you to come, you're my friend." Angela started heading to her class, "Gotta get to class, see you tomorrow?"

"Sure," Amy said, "See you then."

Angela felt happier on her way to class thinking over time all of the girls in the group would have a good influence on Amy and build her esteem so she would value herself more. She realized she had to be patient, you can't make everything better in one conversation. You have to invest in people she told herself, and over time Amy will grow, she thought. It takes long term commitment and long term love. She also wrote a little reminder in her notebook to ask Shonice to sit next to Amy and also ask her to hang out with her when she can. She laughed to herself thinking about how Shonice could chase those powerless and worthless feelings right out of Amy. She thought in her seat in class waiting for it to start how tough Shonice was, and how funny, she laughed to herself again, this time her body moved and she laughed a little out loud.

Her friend next to her asked, "What's so funny?"

"Nothing." Angela said with a smile. She thought of the energy and spunk Shonice adds to the group, and smiled thinking of what she would have told Amy at lunch. She made a note to have Amy ask Shonice for advice sometime about that boy. She was in Janet Novak's (the teacher Janet who joined her morning group) English class and missed everything she opened with being so deep in thought and fought mentally to get back into what was going on.

The next morning Emily started off the meeting. "I have a question I wanted to ask you." But before she could ask it someone else asked in friendly tone, "I want to ask you when you and Ethan are going to start actually going out?" There was a small round of laughter.

"Ethan and I are just fine, who knows." Angela answered. "So Emily, what did you want to ask?"

"I know we've kind of talked about this, but I wanted ask you about fear. How do you deal with fear?"

"Fear is our biggest enemy," Angela answered. "It is the main thing keeping us from blossoming the way we could. Without it, we would live life with total abandon, glorious and powerful."

"How do you beat it?" One of the guys in the group asked.

"First, don't let yourself cling to worry as the mechanism to deal with it. Just use the other things we've talked about, the meditation, self-talk. You have to practice certain things to have victory. Worry can't be our 'go to' defense mechanism. So stop it at the source. Just like with negative feelings, recognize it, tell yourself not to worry. Realize just about every philosophical discipline tells you not to worry about things you can't control. Use the meditative technique, catch the thought, recognize it, send it out, on its way.

Also, prayer is very important. Pray for help and strength to overcome your fears. Along the same lines, trust also that the universe will turn as it should, if something is meant to be it will happen, if not, it won't. We do have a part in that with what we do, but ultimately it is beyond us. We can have a big effect though by acting positively to solve something or attain a goal. We can interact but not control totally, so don't worry about it. All will happen as it will. Work on attaining your personal peace as we have talked about before and you will just flow with your life as you go. Stay on your path and you will get where you need to go."

Emily added, "You also tell me to do everything needful and let it all go. Do all you have the power and resources to do and then relax and let it flow."

"And don't be concerned or live for outcomes," Shonice added.

"Don't be attached to outcomes," another voice was heard saying.

"Scary, you guys are listening." Angela said with a smile.

Someone else asked. "What outcomes?"

Emily started to answer and then stopped.

"Go on Em," Angela said.

Emily beamed. "What's going to happen in the future. Any expectancy. Anything that comes next. Obsessing about the future instead of living in the present, living in the moment. We have to plan well, set goals, do all we can in the strength and time that given us and let it go, don't worry about the future. Like Ang says, trust the source."

"The source?" Someone asked from the crowd.

"The Supreme being, what's ultimately controlling everything."

"Like that line from the book, The Lord of the Rings," Ben, one of the guys from the group said, chiming in for the first time. "All we have to think about is what to do with the time that's been given us." The group all looked at him. He was uneasy about all the attention and also was worried his idea was going to sound stupid and wished he didn't say it. "You know, Gandalf told Frodo." Everyone was still focused on him, listening. "In...the book"

"That's a cool example, I love those books." Angela said, breaking in to help him out of the spotlight. Thanks, uh..."

"Ben," he answered somewhat sheepishly.

"Thanks Ben, very cool."

Someone else spoke up, "Out of sight man, very cool."

Shonice added, "That's right, doing what you can with what you have, is all that matters. That's all you're responsible for."

Angela's heart was warmed by how everyone chimed in to help Ben out of his predicament in the spotlight. She loved the spirit of what was happening here. There was a unity, a unity of love. The people here weren't playing at friendly, they weren't acting and then feeling good about themselves for it. These people seemed to be truly interested in bettering themselves and their world. They were into loving their fellow human beings merely for the sake of doing that, not as some kind of spiritual salve rubbed on themselves once a week and then living a completely different life, totally unaware of this difference. That kind of thing, Angela thought, is so dangerous and unfortunately so prevalent. She was also so proud of Em, watching her grow and be so joyful.

"I remember," Clair added, "You also talked about taking action as an antidote for fear."

"Cool, yeah I remember." Angela said.

"Yeah," Sharon a student who had been there from the beginning said, "You said that thoughtful action remedies fear."

"Why?" Janet added, the teacher in her coming out.

Sharon thought for a minute then added, "Because you'll extinguish fear because you're either planning a resolution to what's making you anxious or you're finishing it, which takes care of it for sure. Either relaxes you."

"So, by even planning a solution you're taking action, and that calms you down." Emily said.

"Yes," Angela said. "Something's on your mind, bothering you, plan a solution and then do it. Take the steps necessary. But you've got to ultimately remedy the habit of it or something else will take its' place, and that would be fear and doubt. And that takes us back to where we started. Fear paralyzes. Action is the opposite and the antidote. So if something is making you fearful, plan the steps to combat it. Planning gives you peace, makes you optimistic because you see a structure to your goal or how to make your future happen.

Let's say you're fearful about success in school. First tell yourself that you are going to take action to solve it. You feel fearful, attack. Find the resources in people, books, and journals, for example and learn about how to have better study habits. Think about your weak subject areas and get the help you need. It's out there.

But by taking steps not only will it start you on your way to your goal, it will give you peace and help keep fear and anxiety away because it makes this future you want become real to you, you will feel your dream becoming tangible. Remind yourself how smart you are, and what great potential we all have to do what we want if we want it badly enough, you can't stop a person like that," Angela enthusiastically.

"What if you are worried about money?" Sara, who works in the school's office, and joined the group with Janet asked.

"That's a big one," Angela said. "We have to be sure we are separating needs from wants first. People can be discontented about money and then want more and are stressed about it, wishing they had more as others do around them. First we have to be sure we have a right perspective, being blown away about what we do have. Most of us in this country are not going to be without adequate shelter or clean water as many around the world are today, as an example. And we have to be sure we are not just pining for more money and living for that as our major life goal. There is nothing wrong with wanting to make more money, I just disagree with seeing it as the only major goal in a person's life and thinking that the total pursuit of it will bring lasting joy, harmony and contentment.

But with that, it's the same strategy. Take action. Plan what you can do to change your situation that is worrying you. Write them down, check them off as you go. Again, seek help from people whose life's work is to help people financially plan better. They can help with things like making a budget, and planning for the future. Remind yourself of the strategies you came up with in your plan during your self-talk. During all of this surround yourself with positive people. Positive people will encourage you and they will also be action oriented and will help keep your feet to the fire, as my mom would say, so you complete what you set out to do.

Related to money, you may need or want a change in career. This is just as important for adults because they will probably have to reinvent themselves, doing something new and different, chances are, sometime in their lives. First, find out what you're good at and then think of what you want to do and be in your new career. There are even tests you can take to see what is a good fit for you as a career. Then plan a way to get there."

7

For Em

Tuesday started out as any day would, bright sunny morning, clear sky. Angela sat on her porch where she was eating breakfast as she sometimes does. There was no group today, she moved it to three days a week so she could have some free time in the mornings.

She looked out in the yard and saw the sun streaming through the trees, the beams splitting through the branches. She stopped eating and put her fork down. She walked off the porch and toward the trees she was watching. She stood under them and looked up and watched the rays streaking through the gaps in the leaves and branches. She held her arms up and began to slowly turn, the shimmering rays spiraling all around her like a warm kaleidoscope.

After breakfast she walked to school feeling great. Her time had set the right tone to start the day. At school everything seemed as it always did, kids milling all around heading to classes, standing by lockers talking, teachers getting set up in their rooms. Something was different though to Angela but she could not quite figure it out. Then she realized. "Em. Where's Em?" she looked around where she would normally be but didn't see her. She started to ask people if they saw Emily anywhere and no one had. She finally found Shirley Thompson, Emily's next door neighbor, at her locker.

"Hey Shirley." Angela said, tapping her on the shoulder.

"Hey." She grabbed her books and closed the locker.

"Have you seen Emily?" "Oh man, didn't anyone tell you, she's not here, her brother got killed in Vietnam."

"What! No. No one told me. Gotta go."

Angela raced down the hall and out of the school and ran over to Emily's house as fast as she could. She ran up to the house, knocked on the door. No one answered. She kept knocking but no one was home. There was no car in the driveway either. She went to the house next door and knocked on their door.

A woman opened the door. "Can I help you?"

"Yes, I'm Angela Morgan, Emily's best friend. Do you know where she is?"

The woman looked reluctant and had a sad look on her face.

"Please tell me. She is my best friend, I care about her very much. If anything happened to her I have to know. I know about her brother. Please."

The woman looked pained to speak and also as if she shouldn't be saying anything. "She, took it badly, she, just left. No one knows where she is."

"Where are her parents? They're out looking for her right?"

The woman hesitated again, the pained look back on her face. "They went to her sisters," She lowered her voice, "her aunt's house."

"What!" Angela threw her arms down disgusted.

She went back to the school to get her bag and her lunch so she could go looking for Emily. She ran into Ethan without even realizing it. "Oh! Hi. Gotta run."

"What's going on?" Ethan asked.

"Emily's brother was killed and she's gone, ran away." Angela was working on holding it together. "I've got to find her!"

Ethan held Angela's shoulders. "It's going to be okay, I' go with you. We'll take my car, c'mon." The two ran down the hall, people turning around wondering what was going on. They went out into the parking lot and to Ethan's car.

When they were driving off there was a strange silence, everything quiet for a moment. Angela looked at Ethan.

"Thanks."

The silence felt strange. This was the first time they were alone together like this. But Angela couldn't stay focused on that long.

"I am totally freaked out. I am so worried about her."

"Me too, we'll find her," Ethan said confidently.

"This is really cool of you." Angela said.

"No problem."

After a short time and more silence, Ethan sensed her worry and pain, and added, "We'll find her," he said, "Don't worry."

The two drove around all day but there was no sign of Emily anywhere. No one had seen her or heard anything. They went to the police station and tried to report her missing. They told them it had not been long enough and also that only her parents could do that.

They got in the car after leaving the police station. When they were driving off Angela folded her arms and slumped into the seat and said, "Where are you Em?" tears streaming down her cheeks. Then she added, "They were not very helpful either. And then didn't seem to care at all either."

After a short pause Ethan looked at her and smiled. "Well...they're probably not exactly your biggest fans." He paused.

Angela thought about it. "Oh, the protest." She said.

"Ohhh yea," Ethan said smiling at her.

Thinking about it during the short silence caused an outburst of laughter in both of them.

Ethan turned the Angela, "It's good to see you laugh."
They drove around all day and until 11:00 that night.
They both decided to head home. Ethan dropped Angela
off at home, and offered to do the same tomorrow if she
wanted.

She got out of the car and walked over to the driver's side
window. His window was down. She put both her hands
on the door. "You're awesome, thanks." Angela said.

"Get some sleep." Ethan told her.

"I'm not going to sleep," Angela said.

She pointed at him as she walked away, her arms
outstretched and smiled, "But you mister, you get some
sleep."

"Yes sir." He said smiling back.

Angela's mom came out of the door. She knew what had
happened and as they stopped home to tell her earlier
what was going on. She thanked Ethan, put her arms
around Angela to comfort her and then closed the door.

Angela knew there was no way that she could even lay
down in her bed, let alone sleep as she was so worried
about her friend. She felt so good about Ethan and
thought for a moment what a great guy he was. But she
couldn't focus on her happiness now, she had to find
Emily. She went back outside, she had to have some air.
She sat in her favorite spot when she couldn't sleep,

against the wooden porch, arms wrapped around her legs. After an hour, she sat eyes open, unmoved.

The silence was broken by the crunching sound of tires on the gravel driveway leading up the house. Angela lived in a home built around the turn of the century, with a big porch in the front of it, and large gravel driveway leading up to it.

It was Ethan. He got out and closed the door and sat down the exact same way Angela was sitting. They sat for a few minutes in silence. Angela rested her head on Ethan's shoulder.

"You remembered that I said that this is my favorite spot when I can't sleep." She paused. They sat together; the only sound was crickets chirping. "Thanks."

"There's no place I'd rather be," He said. Then Ethan turned and looked at Angela. "There's no other place I could be."

She turned to look at him, taken by what he said, staring at him. He smiled at her.

They both were dozing an hour later, sitting in the same spot when they heard the phone ring in the house. They both jumped at the ringing of the phone. It scared both of them, not only because it startled them, but because a phone ringing in the middle of the night is always an unsettling experience. Angela seemed reluctant to answer it but she did. It was her friend Linda. Angela was filling Ethan in as Linda was telling her what happened.

"It's Linda." Angela listened intently to what she was saying. "She's at a party, and she thinks she saw Emily there." She stopped as she listened. "What?!" Angela looked right at Ethan. "And she's really wasted." Angela looked much more intense now. "Linda,...Linda. Where are you?" Angela looked frustrated as Linda went on. "Linda, listen to me, where are you? What's the address?" Angela started writing down the address quickly. "Okay, I'm coming over, now." She hung up the phone. "Here's the address, let's go.

The two rushed out of the house and got in the car. They got to the house. Cars were parked everywhere, the street, driveway, even on the grass. They got out of the car and could hear the noise inside. When they opened the front door the noise level doubled, and then were hit by all the smoke, the smell and the confusion. They could hardly see anything. It was dark, the only light source being from lava lamps and some black lights placed over posters on the wall. Angela was thinking, "Where in the world is Linda, and how am I going to find her?" They were trying to get past the people and through the haze when they heard Linda shout,

"Angela!"

Linda seemed to come out of nowhere and grab Angela.

"This way. She's in here."

She led them through the house, down a hall through the maze of people, sitting, standing, lying on the floor, to a room where Emily was sitting on a couch with several

people. Angela knelt down in front of the couch by
Emily. She brushed her hair out of her face, it was wet
and matted down. She tried to see her eyes.

"Em? Em?"

She wasn't conscious. Angela stood up and gently started
to lift her off the couch. Ethan came over to the other side
of her to help.

A guy by Emily looked indignant. "Hey man, What do
you think you're doing?" He put his hand on Angela's
arm. "She's with us, man." Angela took his arm off of her
and kept lifting Emily. He reached again to grab her arm,
Angela pulled it away and glanced at him. "Don't even."

Ethan and Angela lifted Emily off the couch.

"Whoa. Ooh. Who are you," the guy went on, "the heat
or something?"

The two got her up and began carrying her away.

"Hey, she's with us, man, I told you!" They heard him
shouting as they moved away, two other voices chiming
in.

Angela and Ethan ignored them and worked faster to get
Emily out of there. They moved quickly to get her into
the crowd, and out, and hopefully lose her new "friends"
on the couch and avoid turning this into a brawl. The
confusion hid them in the mass of people, loud music,
and thick smoke, and then they could hear the guy on the

couch yelling at them, getting closer as they went. They felt as though they were going too slowly. Ethan finally picked Emily up and carried her in his arms. They started to move faster and weave their way through the crowd.

"Emily had definitely picked the wrong crowd to hang out with," Angela thought.

They could see the door when suddenly someone stood right in their path. He looked down at Ethan.

"This is totally uncool, she's with us." Somehow the guy on the couch and his two friends made it to the door before them.

"She's sick," Ethan said, "We have to get her out of here and get her help."

"You're going nowhere." The guy in front was very tall and very wide. They couldn't even see around him.

Angela stepped in front of Ethan and looked up at him. "My friend is really sick, she's completely passed out. She's no fun to you dead."

They said nothing. Then the big guy who blocked their path said, "Hey, wait, man,.. you're the protest chick."

"What?" The guy from the couch said.

"The chick we saw on tv, man. When they emptied the schools and marched."

"Yeah, far out, that is her," the other friend said.

"Who cares," The guy from the couch protested. "That chick's mine."

"Shut up," the big guy said. He looked at Angela. "She took on the man, and won, shut 'em down. She's cool." He waved his hand. "You can go."

"What!?" The couch guy blurted out.

"I told you to shut up," the big guy growled.

Angela wasn't waiting around and grabbed Ethan by the arm and led them out. They got in the car and put Emily in the back seat and Angela got in with her. They didn't want to linger there so Angela checked Emily the best she could as they drove away.

Angela brushed her hair away from her face again. "Oh, Em," Angela looked worried, and then spoke in a soft voice. "What did you do?"

"I'm headed for the hospital," Ethan said.

"Thanks," Angela answered.

They got to the hospital emergency entrance and got Emily inside. Angela couldn't believe how awful it was to see them lift Emily's limp body, completely unconscious, onto the gurney. She put her hands over her mouth as they lifted her. She looked dead. Ethan came behind her and put his hand on her shoulder. Angela put her hand on his as the nurses and paramedics worked hastily to get her back. Angela felt helpless as they wheeled her away and back. Angela ran after them, a nurse stopped them at the entrance of the room.

"You can't come in," and she closed the door behind her.

Angela and Ethan watched as they put a tube with an oxygen mask over Emily's face. All the frenetic activity in the room made Angela more upset for her friend. Another doctor pushed past them and in. "Excuse me," he said, and went in the room and began calling out orders.

A nurse came behind Ethan and Angela and told them they would have to go the waiting area.

As they sat down the nurse told them that they would let them know as soon as they could.

A few minutes later a woman in scrubs and a clip board came up to them and sat down.

"Are you part of her family?" She asked.

"No." Angela answered. "Her friend," she said despondently, thinking of Emily's family.

"Where is her family?" The nurse asked.

"I don't know," Angela said. "I can try calling them." "Yes, that would help, the woman said." She handed Angela a clip board with a personal information form on it. "And if you could fill this out as best you can that would help. Angela took the clipboard. "I'll try calling her parents." "Thank you," the woman said, and walked away.

Angela began to write on the paper then put the pen down in her lap and dropped her hands on it and breathed out heavily.

"She'll be okay." Ethan said, and he put his hand on hers.

Angela called Emily's parents and woke them up. She told her mother what happened and where they were. An hour later Emily's mother walked through the door looking expressionless. Ethan stood up to greet her. She didn't say anything, so Angela spoke to break the awkward silence.

"We haven't heard anything yet."

Her mother just nodded and walked over to the nurse's station. Ethan looked at Angela. They both watched as Emily's mother talked to the nurse. They could only make out a few words at a time. They could hear her say that she is her mother. Then a few random words after that, and the nurse telling her that they will let her know the minute they do, and to Angela's amazement she left.

"What?" Angela breathed out slowly. They watched the front door close. "She's leaving?" Angela went on in disbelief.

She got up and walked over to the nurse's station. "Hi, is she coming back, do you know?"

"I don't think so," the nurse said. "I told her we would call her when we knew anything."

Angela slowly walked back to her seat by Ethan, in disbelief of she just witnessed. She sat down and breathed out hard. "I don't believe it."

"I can't imagine it either."

"Poor Em." Angela looked around at the waiting room. "How much pain she must carry around all the time." She sat straight ahead, staring at nothing.

"And you'd never even know." Ethan added.

"Yeah" Angela said, in a groggy voice, the tiredness overtaking her.

They both were in a half sleeping state when the nurse came up to them in their chairs two hours later. Ethan was already awake and gently shook Angela awake. "Ang, the nurse is here," he said softly. Angela slowly opened her eyes feeling dazed, and saw the nurse. She remembered where they were seeing the nurse and sat up. "How is she?"

"Your friend has been moved."

"Where, how is she?"

"She's alive, the nurse said. I can't tell you more than that."

"What, why?" Angela asked.

"Only her immediate family."

"This can't be happening. Can we visit her?" Angela asked.

"Not tonight. She's in intensive care." With that, the nurse left.

Angela looked frustrated. "I can't believe we can't find out how she is."

"Why don't we try to contact her mother?" Ethan offered.

"She'd probably not tell me, and I have to know how she is."

Angela sat in thought for a second. "Hold it," she said quickly, "Here come with me." She just saw a doctor leave the ICU. She watched where he was headed and ran up and cut him off as he was about to turn a corner. She stood right in front of him.

"Excuse me doctor. I am with Emily in ICU, I brought her in, sat here all night waiting. How is she?"

The doctor looked startled, jumping back slightly. "Well, she's stable now. She overdosed on several substances. We're monitoring her closely." He went to move around Angela. She steeped in front of him again. "Is she conscious?"

He looked at her surprised by her forthrightness. "Uh, no, but we're hoping she will be soon. Now I've got to go." And he stepped around her and moved quickly down the hall.

Angela stood there thinking, "Man, at least we know something."

"You're what's something, "Ethan said, amazed at how she found out. "C'mon, I'll take you home. There's nothing more we can do here. We'll come back later."

"Thanks," Angela said. "And thanks for coming and staying here all night."

"Wouldn't want to be anywhere else." And they held hands and walked out.

8

The Waiting is the Hardest Part

They did move Emily to a regular room when she was out of danger, so they could visit and sit with her. Everyday Angela and Ethan visited Emily with all the free time they had. She was unconscious though, in a drug induced coma. The doctors said that they had no idea when she would come out of it, if ever.

Angela had not seen Emily's mother at all in the hospital to visit Emily. Angela thought perhaps she came during the day while she was at school. She hated seeing Emily lying there, tubes in her arms and a tube in her nose. It hurt the same every time she came there. In two days Emily hadn't moved at all. Angela was slumped over the railing of the bed watching Emily, talking to her, praying, hoping she heard her, gently stroking her arm.

She heard someone enter the room. Figuring it was the nurse she didn't turn around. She was surprised when she saw it was Emily's mother.

"Hi," Angela said.

Her mother said hello back and sat in another chair beside the bed. She had a small book in her hand that she held tightly. Her mother didn't say anything beyond that.

"She hasn't moved at all," Angela offered softly.

Her mother adjusted herself in the chair and squeezed the book again tightly. Angela looked at the book and then at her, her mother noticing. Her mother looked down at the book again and then at Emily lying there in the bed. She looked like she was trying to say something. She opened her hands and laid the book in them flat. She kept looking at the book as she spoke in a soft voice.

"She," her voice trailed off. "She wrote in this book." She didn't seem to be able to go any further.

Angela tried to help her. "She kept a diary?"

"I didn't know that she had." Her mother nodded slowly, still looking down. "She really cares about you, appreciates you, what you do for her. She has never been so happy since she met you."

Angela smiled. "She also wrote about how she thinks we don't care about her and ignore her, and how painful it is for her. And how much she still loves us, especially me." Angela took her hand. Her mother looked at Emily. "She wrote that she still loves me and wishes I would..." tears started running down her mother's face. "She wishes I would love her too."

"She's a great kid and she loves you very much, she's told me." Angela said.

Emily's mother looked at her. Angela nodded yes and smiled. "She wants nothing more than to be close to you."

Her mother looked at Emily again and said, "She also said she thought all the joy was gone from me and wished there was something she could do to get it back for me, see me happy."

Angela squeezed her hand and smiled at her. "You can."

Emily's mother stared off. "My son is dead. My daughter is dead. I feel dead."

Angela reached over and hugged Emily's mother. Her mother cried hard as she held her. Two of the nurses heard her crying and came to the doorway and saw Angela consoling her. They knew the pain this woman was in and stood motionless at the scene teary eyed.

"She's not gone yet," Angela reassured her. Emily's mother looked at her. "She's not gone yet," Angela said again. "There's always hope."

After they stayed for a little while longer they both left. Angela told Emily's mother to please let her know if anything changes and the hospital calls her, and also if she needs anything from her as well.

The next day Emily's mother called. Angela's mother answered and immediately went down to the school to find Angela. The school called Angela to the office and her mother was standing there by the secretary's desk.

"She's awake!" Her mother said excitedly, she's awake!" They hugged and started hurriedly out of the school.

Angela stopped abruptly. "Wait!" We have to get Ethan. They had the school call him out of class and the three of them went down to see Emily.

When they got there Emily was sitting up. She looked weak and groggy but was awake and smiled when they walked in. Her mother was there sitting beside the bed holding her hand. Emily was smiling from her mother's attention.

"Hey Kiddo, you gave us quite a scare." Angela said.

"Sorry," Emily said.

Angela hugged her and then Ethan did.

Emily smiled at them. "I heard how you guys came and got me, very cool." She paused while she slowly swallowed the water the nurse gave her. Then she sat back looking tired, dark circles under her eyes. "Thanks." Angela put her hand on her. "You just rest. You have to get better. We'll come over right after school, okay?"

"Kay." Emily answered back.

Angela knew that she had to get back to school and didn't want to interfere with Emily's time with her mother. Everyone left and they were alone. The room was quiet except for the noise outside the room. They sat quietly for a few minutes. Then Emily said, "Sorry." She looked like she was going to cry. Her mother got up and hugged her. She held her tight.

"I'm sorry too baby," She brushed her hair with her hand.

"I want you to know that I love you very much."

"I love you too."

A nurse who was walking in to take Emily's vitals paused at the door when she saw them, smiled and left.

Angela was glad to be back in school the next day, the routine and being busy was going to help her forget what happened yesterday. She was working on the mental practice she taught the others, when such negative thoughts came, such as seeing her friend unconscious on that couch, or the scenes at the hospital, to recognize them and then let them go, before they took hold of her. Angela noticed someone was rushing to catch up to her in the hallway as everyone was heading to their classes. She turned.

"Hey Angela."

"Hey Ben, how are you?"

"Good, really enjoyed the group last week. I want to come all the time."

Angela noticed he was a lot more comfortable now than when he brought up his comment using 'Lord of the Rings' in the group last week. She liked seeing him that way.

"I wanted to ask you about fear like we talked about."

"It's our worst enemy," Angela said as they walked down the hall.

"Yeah," Ben said. "But what about stuff we can't control, that's what gets me."

"Don't worry about what you can't control, it does no good. Everything will happen as it should. Remember when Gandalf told Frodo that there are other forces at work here for good, greater than we are, and how that was a comforting thought?"

"Wow, you knew that, cool."

Angela had to turn the corner and head down a different direction. "It's true, and should comfort you. Remember that, it was good advice, repeat it to yourself when you start to worry. We can talk more about it later." She said as she headed down a different hallway.

"Take care," She called out to him.

"You too," Ben said waving his hand.

In class that next period the seat next to Angela where Emily normally sat looked sadly empty. Angela felt the bad feeling coming over her, stopped it and thought, I miss her but she's alive and well, and man I'm grateful for that.

After school Angela visited Emily at home. When she got there Emily was sitting in bed, propped up, staring ahead. Angela sat on the side of the bed. "Hey, how are you feeling?"

'Eh, Good, I guess."

Emily looked tired and drawn but had much more color in her face then the last time she saw her and Angela was so glad for that. "Bored," Emily added. "I want to get out of here," she said. "I'm going crazy from laying here."

"That's good," Angela said with a smile, "Means you're getting better. When can you get out of here?"

Emily looked up at the ceiling and breathed out, slapping her arms down on the bed.

"Doctor says I can go back to school tomorrow, Yea."

"Are you sleeping ok?"

Emily began to tear up. She looked to the side, out the window. "Kind of."

"The dreams?" Angela asked.

"Yeah," Emily put her hands flat against her face and then ran them up and through her hair as she breathed out hard. "I see him," she paused, "I see Brian. He's in uniform. It's all white behind him and he's waving." Emily slowly waved her arm, gesturing goodbye, tears sliding slowly down her cheek. "It's torture."

"Sorry," Angela leaned over and hugged Emily.

"I know, though this won't last forever." Angela said as she hugged her. I know it won't." She slowly swayed side to side as she hugged her. "I promise."

Emily sat back and sniffed hard, trying to breath because of her crying.

"It will get better, over time." Angela said. She put her hand on Emily's hand. "It won't always be like this."

They sat in silence for a while, Emily much calmer, and tired from bad sleep. Still propped up but leaning back against her pillow, she spoke slowly and softly. "I remembered what you said." She paused, staring at the ceiling. Angela sat quiet smiling softly at her. "I remember you said, when we talked about it in the group, wait for the flower that will bloom. You said when we have hard times, be patient, wait for the flower that will bloom, some good will come out it." Still looking up she seemed to relax more as she spoke. "You said, wait for it." She sat there for a minute thinking. "I clung to that when I found out what happened to Brian." She paused. After a minute she looked at Angela. "I held onto that for dear life," she said. Angela smiled at her. "I also clung to what I had in you guys, my friends, you were there. Thanks."

"We love you."

"I know," Emily said smiling.

"It's great about your mom."

Emily smiled. "I know, it's been great."

Emily sat there for a minute and then looked at Angela again. "A flower has bloomed."

Angela smiled, "Sure has."

9

Here Comes the Sun

The next day the group was really into the discussion and Angela was happy that so many people were chiming in and giving thoughtful impressions. She was also pleased that everyone was respecting each other and letting each other finish, and that they were all truly listening to each other and interested in what the other person was saying. They were talking about having perspective in life and how important it is for harmony. Perspective meaning having the right appreciation for what you have and focusing in that direction instead being focused on what you don't have.

"Okay," Angela said. "Let's see what we've talked about because we've covered a lot of ground. We talked about seeing and appreciating all that we have. We are in the land of abundance. Most of the world lives with much, much less. We said how we should really stop and look, and be amazed by how much we really have, all we need and more. And how we tend to be dissatisfied and want more instead of being content and blown away, as I like to put it, with the abundance we have been given. We talked about this some when we talked about anxiety and money. We said also how when people are fixed on the accumulation of things rather than fixed on personal peace and peace or harmony with the world, possessions becomes the total life goal but will never satisfy us. And many of you said you don't want to be part of that world and I don't either."

Ben spoke up. "And that leads to endless chasing after the wrong things."

"Cool Ben, yeah. And what did I say happens to people when they have chased this as Ben said all their lives, and when they get older and look back on it, what do they see, what do they feel?"

"Bad." Someone called out.

Summer, a girl in the group raised her head up out of the crowd. "They realize, hopefully, that it was all for nothing."

"Yeah. Thanks, the end is despair," Angela added. "And it's just like with all of the other things we discuss here. First you attain personal peace with yourself and the world, then you go and you want to share it with someone else and help them achieve the same. You want to make a difference in your world."

Shonice spoke up, "We could have world peace if everyone did that."

The whole group resonated with her comment.

"Yes, that is so important. We have to know the potential in us. This is possible. This is not some pipe dream, or wishful, way out thinking. This could happen. Peace in ourselves would lead to peace in our world. This is a potential reality, if we all get together." Angela sat up, passion in her voice, her hands gesturing more excitedly. "This is what this whole thing is about. A life worth living. A life of passion, a life of peace, a full life, where you are jazzed about what's around you, and its infectious, your love for everything is infectious, your love for the world, your love for people. You won't destroy what you love!"

People were calling out cheers and agreements all excitedly and happily. The group was buzzing with feeling.

"Yeah!!!" Someone yelled out.

"Preach it sister!" Shonice called out, a big smile on her face.

"Think of the unity in the world," Angela said happily, "What would there be to fight about?" Angela stopped and looked at everyone as she said it, her hands stretched out in front of her.

"Everybody would work toGETHER!" Shonice said with emphasis.

"Right on!" Someone else called out.

Lloyd, who usually carries his guitar with him, started playing some solid riffs on his guitar as if on cue from the song, "Let's Work Together." He had his electric guitar with him and his friend in his band plugged it into the huge portable radio they had. He and all of the other guys in the band began drumming in unison on their books. The music sounded great as Lloyd jammed hard and loud and everyone started clapping as Lloyd sang the song, "Let's Work Together", by Canned Heat.

Lloyd then stood up and jammed the solo part of the song as his friends continued drumming hard on their books, while people were dancing around them.

Angela was teary eyed as she saw the very dream of her life happening right in front of her in their little corner of the world. It was a great moment. Everyone was hugging each other and dancing around, lifting each other up, and smiling as they never have before. The song was perfect, about being united, working together, and standing together, and it includes everyone.

The music was attracting other students who looked up to the hill and heard it but couldn't see what was happening. The song having such a strong melody, and was playing so loudly, students kept coming up, so Lloyd kept playing on.

At the end of the next meeting Angela mentioned something she always wanted to do with all of them next time. "I wanted to ask you guys if you would like to do something that fits perfectly with what we have been talking about. We have been talking a lot about keeping a better perspective and appreciating more what's around us and what we have. We also talked about the inner peace we're always talking about," she said with a laugh, "and how to share it with the world, and how that unity would create a peaceful world. Well..." she hesitated, smiling again, "I had an idea and I wanted to see if you guys were hip to it or not."

The group saw how excited she was and many were smiling in anticipation of it.

Angela went on. "An Ancient Chinese philosopher once said, 'How can you complain about the day when you weren't even up to see the sun rise.' So," she said looking at everyone. "Let's all mediate on that, see what we come with tomorrow as we watch the sun rise."

The group was buzzing with conversation about it.

Angela raised her arms up so she could be heard. "And...Since tomorrow is Saturday, why don't we meet at the beach and do this?"

Now the group was really animated. Angela was also, slightly rocking as she went on.

"And...since the music was so far out,"

The crowd got louder acknowledging Lloyd and his band.

"I wanted to ask Lloyd and the boys to do some music for us." Angela spoke loudly through the cheers. "Sunrise music, can you also play some acoustic sunrise music?"

The group got louder. Lloyd knew he couldn't be heard anymore over the din so he did a thumbs up then a peace sign with a smile.

Angela threw him a kiss and said, "Wow, cool, see everyone tomorrow."

The loud crowd began to disperse and go their own ways to class all a buzz over meeting tomorrow.

Ethan and Angela picked up Emily at her house and they drove to the beach together. When they got there it was still completely dark, no moon out that night. They found out that some of the group had been there all night, cooking and hanging out. They could see some fires going on the beach as they walked up from the parking lot. It was so fun walking onto the beach from the parking lot hearing everybody talking and milling around, having a great time. People were sitting on blankets, some were sleeping, some were by the water staring out; a couple sat together, one of them pointing out into the distance.

After a little while Angela got everybody together. She wanted to be sure to start before it started to get light. Everyone huddled together, relaxed and happy.

"This is so cool how everybody came out. We are here to have a groovy time, to cultivate the mind to attain the enlightenment and peace we talked about last time, and change the world."

Cheers were heard all over.

"It's also about that change of perspective we talked about also. Whose ever started a day like this before?"

"Yeah man," Lloyd said,

Ben added, "Yeah, this was all here man, and I never noticed it like this."

"And remember," Angela said. "People are going to say you're crazy for doing stuff like this, they are going to call me crazy. That doesn't matter. You have to hold on to what you know, life can be like this, it can be our reality, it's our choice. Break from the mold of how people say it should be. We are here to lead, not fight with them, to show them a better way."

"We also have to stick together. We are strong together." Shonice said.

"Here it comes!" Someone shouted.

First there was a glow forming on the edge of the shoreline. The sound of the waves accompanying the moment. Seagulls flew overhead and out into the scene being lit by the light coming up on the horizon. Part of a gleaming ball that was the sun was starting to show its shape.

"Go Lloyd baby!" Shonice called out.

Right on cue Lloyd starting playing his 12 string acoustic guitar, and it seemed to echo over the water. He had another guitar playing with him so the sound was full and strong. Lloyd starting singing and everyone joined in with him, the glowing ball that was the sun coming up the shoreline.

The song ended and everybody sat and watched it light up a new day. Most were sitting arms wrapped around their knees watching out to sea. Some stood, some were lying on their backs, necks cranked up to see, but everyone was focused and appreciating a new day in a special way.

Angela saw these moments as beautiful additions to each of us, completing a filling up of the whole. She even said later that this morning was a glorious coin dropped in the jars of our souls, filling us up to completion as we move through this journey which is our lives.

When the meeting was getting close to being done, a group of people sat in a circle with Lloyd and were trying to think of all of the songs they could about the sun or sunrise and were having a great time.

Angela stood up and stretched. Ethan stood up also and began to help fold up their blanket. They kept folding the corners and moving closer, until they were standing close together. Angela was holding the blanket and looking out at everyone, all doing their own thing, having fun together. "This was awesome." She said.
Ethan moved closer. "You're awesome.

They stood close staring dreamingly at each other, feeling alone in the universe at the moment. They moved slowly together and kissed. They stood together and held their kiss. They stood unmoved until they heard a building of cheers and clapping and people calling out. "Yeah," "Alright," Some whistling, and then Lloyd said with a smile, "It's about time." The two eventually broke their kiss but still held each other tightly as the approval rose louder. The two never took their eyes off of each other while it went on, telling each other with their eyes all that hey've been wanting to say but didn't until now.

10

Transforming the Mundane

Angela reflected on the day later at home and was so grateful it was allowed to happen. She thought back on how well everyone got along and were all growing toward their goal, herself included. She couldn't believe how her whole day was transformed and imagined everyone's was. She thought of how everyday could be that way if we do what we did today in some small way.

She remembered the day she once was getting ready for school, and remembered what she did one time when she was little. She just opened the door and just ran around the house, but she did it with an abandon, a free and flowing spirit. She remembered and smiled reflecting on it, remembering the feeling as she ran, the way she laughed, how she felt when she got inside. Just one trip around was all she did, but what a trip!

She put her hands on the window sill and imagined herself as a little girl running around the house that great day, even hearing her mother calling her as she ran, calling to her that her breakfast was ready. She savored it, smiled, gently biting her lower lip as she always did for as long as she could remember, always before launching on an idea, and then started down the stairs and out the front door.

As she was coming around the house she heard a voice call her name.

'Ang!"

't was Em.

"Hey!" Angela said stopping.

"What are you doing girl?!"

"Running around the house."

"Why?"

"Transforming the mundane."

Emily lip synched what she said, shaking her head.

"C'mon, bet I beat ya!" Angela said laughing and took off.

Emily ran after her. "You wish!"

They went around the whole house as fast as they could and were really tired at the end when they got back to where they started.

"Man," Angela said breathless, "I am so out of shape."

"It's a discipline girl," Emily said, teasing her, waving her arms around. "You've got to cultivate your body the way you cultivate that mind of yours."

"Shut up," Angela said laughing.

"Hey!" Angela said, suddenly excited.

"Let's go roll down the Fiasconaro's hill!"

"Who? What?" Emily looked confused.

"A hill we used to love to roll down when we were kids. Mr. Fiasconaro would get furious and chase us."

"And you liked that?!"

Angela tossed her head, "Yeah."

"You're crazy."

"Yes."

"And I love it. Let's go!"

The two ran over to the house Angela described, through the grassy yards of other houses that connected them all together, across a street and into another yard to get to the Fiasconaro's.

"We can't just run through this person's yard?" Emily called out.

Angela just ran through and Emily followed laughing. Angela jumped over the row of bushes that separated the Fiasconero' yard and stopped. She looked back at the long row of bushes.

"That used to seem so tall, wow."

They walked to the edge of the hill that encompassed the entire large square shaped yard of the Fiasconaro's. The whole yard was surrounded by that flat edge at the top that they were standing on.

"Man," Angela said looking over the edge and down the hill, "This used to seem huge also."

Emily chuckled, hands on her hips, catching her breath. "Let's do it."

Angela shook out of her thoughts and got back in the spirit. They laid down on their sides and rolled down the bright, green grassy hill, screaming all the way. They did it once and climbed back up. Angela looked down at the house which was quiet when they stared down from the top of the hill.

"Bummer man." Angela said.

"What?"

"Well, no one chased us like when we were kids."

"You don't want them chasing us now, do ya?"

"No," Angela said looking at the house again. "But it's just that it won't happen as it used to anymore." Angela kept staring down at the house.

"So much time has gone by."

"Life moves on." Emily said.

"You're right." Angela said, putting her hand on Emily's shoulder. "Let's head back. That was fun, thanks for letting me do this kiddo, you're awesome."

"Anytime."

Emily had to head home and Angela sat on her porch as she loved to and thought more about transforming the mundane, which had been on her mind all day. She was thinking how that attitude runs the gambit from the wild events of earlier today to even a seemingly small thing. It was so much like appreciation, where she wants to notice more carefully and intentionally all that is around, and create joy from little things as well as big things like the sunrise meeting. A happy and open spirit that looks for appreciation and transformation is easy to please.

Even on the busiest of days as a way to stay appreciative and transform the mundane she would stare up at her favorite tree. She always did it with focus, it was a meditation. For that moment, in that instant, nothing else existed, nothing else was thought about. Even if she was about to be on her way to go somewhere she had to be, she would stop, have that meditative moment of reflection, appreciation of the beauty, notice it, take it in, let everything go, and in the process be realigned as she loves to say, refocused and centered.

Trees were always among her favorite ways to do that but she knew it could be anything in nature. Mountains are great of course, but many things can be used. She remembered one time an unusual example, remarking and reflecting on the way a beautiful curvy, hilly street ran down a hill, watching it hug the terrain and adapt to its intricate curves, making a beautiful scene. But her favorite part was the way at the bottom, from what her eye could see, the road would disappear as it turned, an illusion to the eye. The road at that point looked as though it stopped, or, unseen to the eye, went off to an unknown and mysterious location she imagined.

She always encouraged people to think this way and also to notice the different reactions of people to a simple event. An example she liked to use was to imagine you are in a building and its starts to rain outside. How do people react? Some are glad it's raining and maybe comment on how we needed it. Some might be mad because they just washed their car. All of that is fine but as Angela would say, watch the intentional person's reaction. They may say some of the same things about the rain first but chances are there will be more. They will probably smile over the sound of the rain as it hits the roof. Or perhaps they will talk about the beautiful rhythm of it, or the change in rate as when it starts to pour hard, and gets excited as it does. Angela always says to watch the reaction of such a typical event from a child versus an adult. The differences are illuminating. Another example of what Angela says is the most important thing, never losing your childlike enthusiasm and wonder for things.

Angela was also always quick to point out the difference between "childlike" and "childish." Childlike is great. It involves the unending novelty and wonder of how our world is seen. It is the exuberant expectation of what is to come. It is a true appreciation of all the small things, it's being able to love and trust wholeheartedly and without anticipation of a personal return.

Childish is all together different. That entails arrested development, not growing. Childishness resists growth, abhors change and fights against it. It embodies selfishness as an axiom, and is in immediate conflict with anyone who is viewed as a challenge to it; whether it is the accumulation of money, or power, or position, or pleasure, or whatever else they most desire, and eliminate that threat however is necessary. Angela pointed out that unfortunately that is more of the norm. The good news as she taught is that we can all change. We all have these characteristics in abundance, but the key is to recognize it and work to change ourselves for the better, for us, and for the world's sake.

Angela also made the point that this is very connected to the difference between living the best life and trying to make things better for the world, trying to make a positive difference; as opposed to a life of just grabbing all you can for yourself and eliminating anyone in your way.

11

Jamison and Emerson

Ben ran and caught up with Angela in the hallway. She really liked Ben. He embodied the childlike enthusiasm and wonder for things, and has an innocence about him that makes him precious to her. She aspired to be like him in many regards. Angela also really valued what a devoted friend Ben was turning out to be, and knew how rare that was. She thought back on that day when Ben finally spoke up at the group and gave his now famous "Lord of the Rings" analogy. He has been endearing to Angela's heart ever since.

"Hey, Ang."

Ben then looked a little concerned. "You don't mind if I call you Ang, do ya? Em does."

"Em?"

Angela smiled, "Of course I don't mind."

Emily told Angela later that school day how cute it was to see Ben close to her side trailing along with her. He truly valued her as a friend and teacher. Emily also had been spending some time with Ben and told Angela how she really is learning to value him as a special friend. She told her how she thought he was kind of weird at first but then as she is getting to know him better, in her own words, "Just love the little guy to death." Ben was smaller than most of the kids at the school, but had a huge heart and personality. He turned out also to be fiercely loyal as a friend and both Emily and Angela were grateful for it.

"So have you got anymore of those great quotes from any ancient Chinese Teachers?"

"Sure," she said, thinking about it as they continued walking down the hallway.

"I got one for you Ben. How about, 'A life lived controlled by fear is a tragedy, but a life lived even for one day not controlled by fear is a triumph.'"

"I like it," Ben said, then seemed to be deep in thought.

"That's great. It's like he's talking about letting go. I mean, it's saying like, even if you let go for a really short time and not be ruled by fear it's awesome, no matter how long it was done for, but if you play it safe and are too afraid to try it for your whole life, that's sad no matter what."

"Heavy, buddy, I like how you think."

"It's like you'd be living your whole life in a prison. Here's my class, slap me five sister." Ben held his hand out and Angela slapped down in it.

"Take care brother."

After class Angela saw Ethan walking ahead of her. She sped up and then matched his stride and hooked her arm around his. He was surprised and then smiled at her.

Angela always thought you can tell something about a person by gently surprising them, you may have the

ccasion to get a window into their disposition. Ethan
was kind and gentle and though a little startled displayed
is usual sweet self. She wasn't intending to test him but
is warm response was just more assurance of the man
than was.

Hey," Angela said pushing against him, knocking him a
ttle off balance.

Hey Ang, What's happening?"

Nothing. I did catch myself daydreaming about you in
lass though."

Oh wow cool. Did they notice?"

Yeah."

Really, what happened?"

Well. Mr. Jamison called on me, not once, but twice."

Twice!" Not with Jamison. He's a killer that guy. He
ats students for breakfast. Did he rip into you or what?"

Yes, sort of. He said," Angela lowered her voice and
ropped her chin. "Miss Morgan."

Yes." I said.

Ie looked at me, indignantly, eyes wide. "Am I
isturbing your sleep?"

"'I wasn't sleeping sir,' I said."

"'Then what exactly were you doing?' He said."

"I told him nicely, 'I was daydreaming, sir.'"

Ethan looked shocked. "You told old Ironsides that you weren't sleeping but daydreaming?"

"Yup."

"What did he say to that?"

"He actually asked me what I was day dreaming about"

"What! This is too much. So, what did you tell him?"

Suddenly Ethan's wide eyed amazement and laughter over this changed, his face went deadpan.

Angela smiled and walked quickly ahead of him. Ethan ran up to her smiling, but nervously anticipating her answer. "What did you tell him?"

"Why?" Angela said as she sped up again.

Ethan caught up to her again. "Why?!"

She moved a little bit ahead of him again. He chased aft her.

When he caught up he said, "Because he's crazy, that's why."

Angela stopped and smiled. "I told him I was day dreaming about you," and pointed her finger against his chest.

Ethan grabbed his face with both hands, "Uuuuhhhh, no, I have him today for fifth period. He'll lambaste me. He'll have me for lunch. His favorite thing is to totally roast students in front of the class. That's why everyone hates him, and is terrified of him."

Angela sped up again.

Ethan stood in the same spot, talking to himself. "He doesn't even have any friends on the faculty."

He ran up to her again. "You're loving every minute of this, aren't you?"

"I didn't plan it, honestly. But it is funny how it turned out, isn't it?"

"Oh man, what am I going to tell him?"

"Go toe to toe with him, he loves that." Angela stopped by her class.

"How do you know that?" Ethan asked.

"Because I've seen it."

"How? When?"

"When a student was 10 minutes late."

"Nobody comes into his class late. Everybody knows that. People ditch rather than go late, it's a school rule. Any punishment is better than facing him. What really happened?

"The student really came in late. And, he walked right over to that student, who sat up front."

"Upfront, no chance."

"Yup. And Jamison was ready man, he was foaming," Angela gestured with both hands around her mouth. "He said the student's name while he bobbed his head. You know how he does that?"

"Yes," Ethan said.

"'You're late,' he said.

"Well, before he could start carving into the student, the student said, 'I did it on purpose.'

'On purpose!' Jamison said jerking his head back.

You know how he does that?" She said pushing her finger against his chest again.

"Yeah," Ethan said again.

"'Yes, the student said.'"

"No way in the world would someone do something like that!" Ethan said loudly.

"Seriously. Then the student went on. 'Well, the student said, I want to finish high school, go onto college, get my degree and teach in a school like you do, and I wanted to learn how to handle students when they come in late, so I chose you because you're the best at it.'"

"Oh, c'mon."

"No, its true."

"What did he say?"

"Nothing. He paused for a bit. Then went and shook his head a bit, you know how he does that?"

"Stop it." Ethan said smiling, grabbing her finger in his hand before she could poke him again.

"That's honestly what happened?" Ethan asked as Angela opened the door to her class.

"Yes, honestly." Angela said, finally looking serious. She started to close the door to go into class.

"Wait, I have to know! Who was the student?"

Angela opened the door wide, "Me." And with that she reached up and kissed Ethan hard on the mouth.

The class erupted with cheers and whistles.

Ethan stood tall and frozen in his tracks by the door as it closed. He finally turned and Shonice was standing right behind him waiting to get in, seeing the whole thing.

"I think she's falling for you big time." Shonice said to him with a smile. She started to walk into the classroom, then turned back to him.

"Strap yourself in." She said and walked into class.

After school Angela waited for Ethan as they arranged, on their favorite hill among the trees, near where the group meets. It was a beautiful day, sunny and breezy. Ethan was there first and watched as Angela walked up the hill. The sun's glow lit up the edges of her bright blonde hair as the strong breeze tossed it as she walked. "She is definitely not like anyone else in the world," he thought.

"Hey," Angela said as she came over the hill. She walked over and sat down next to Ethan. She reached over to him. "I want to finish what I started earlier," and she slowly kissed him and held it. She then slowly pulled away, her arms still around his neck. "You're sweet," she said looking into his eyes. Ethan smiled back. They stared at each other, and then Angela remembered something. "Hey, how'd it go with Jamison?"

Ethan looked up, "Ughhh, he had a field day with me. The class loved it though, and so did he."

"I'm sorry, I really wasn't trying to do anything."

She paused. "I probably shouldn't have mentioned you were the reason."

"Ummmhmmm." Ethan hummed in agreement.

"But at the moment I was so filled with thoughts of you. And he asked," she said smiling.

She kissed him again. "Sorry, really."

Ethan nodded. "I think it must be part of the 'strap yourself in phenomenon.'"

"What's that?"

"Shonice was standing there when you kissed me at the doorway of your class and said that she thinks you're falling for me big time, and then right as she was about to close the door she said, 'Strap yourself in.'"

Angela laughed. "Ohhh, Shonice, I love her."

"She's right though." Angela added with a smile.

Ethan grinned as he was rummaging through his backpack. "I bet."

"What have you got for us to hear today?" She asked.

"I have something that I picked out especially for you. I think it really fits with everything you've been saying about the link between us and our environment. And also the descriptions here fit with how you describe your experiences in nature when you work toward centering yourself, toward attaining harmony, and all that good stuff."

Ethan was growing more enthusiastic as he went on. "And I also really thought of you when I read this, the descriptions sounding like what you always say about how the most important thing is to maintain your childlike wonder and enthusiasm."

"Wow, you are so sweet, who is it?"

Ethan took the book out of his bag. "It's Emerson."

"Cool. I love Emerson. Lay it on me."

Ethan opened the book to where he had it marked. Angela smiled watching him.

The day perfectly framed his reading this. It was mid afternoon and the sun was lower and shining through the trees behind them as it began to drop toward its descent.

"Nature" Ethan began.

"...Crossing a bare common, snow puddles, at twilight, under a clouded sky, without having in my thoughts any occurrence of special good fortune, I have enjoyed a perfect exhilaration. I am glad to the brink of fear. In the woods too, a man casts off his years, as the snake his slough, and at what a period soever of life, is always a child. In the woods, is perpetual youth. Within these plantations is God, a decorum and sanctity reign, a perennial festival is dressed, and the guest sees not how he should tire of them in a thousand years. In the woods, we return to reason and faith. There I feel that nothing can befall me in life, -no disgrace, no calamity, (leaving me my eyes,) which nature cannot repair. Standing on the bare ground, -my head bathed by the blithe air, and uplifted into infinite space, -all mean egotism vanishes. I become a transparent eye-ball; I am nothing; I see all; the currents of the Universal Being circulate through me; I am part or particle of God...."

They both looked up and remained silent. They wind picked up as if on cue and whisked its' way through the trees, building up louder as it went. Angela closed her eyes listening and feeling it on her and through her. She opened her eyes and saw Ethan sitting quietly and smiling at her. She scooted closer to him. "I don't want a day to go by where I don't open my eyes and see you."

"Or me you,"

...and they kissed.

12

For Ben

The next day Ben came over and sat down on the grass by Angela during the period for lunch.

"Hey, Ang."

"Hey buddy, what's happening?"

"Not much. Just hanging out."

"Oh, you're trying to eat your lunch, we'll talk another time."

Angela waved her hand. "No, no, stay, no problem, thanks though.

Ben sat down on the grass. "Thanks. I really like the group."

"Cool." Angela said.

"I'm learning a lot, and trying to get it all down. I've been taking notes."

"Wow."

"Yeah, I have them right here." Ben began digging in his backpack.

Angela smiled to herself about how cute he looked digging in his backpack so diligently to find it.

"Here it is," Ben went on. "I wanted to read you some of it if that's okay?"

"Sure," Angela said.

"'Life should be a celebration, and is about seeing and making life an adventure, a joyful and fulfilling experience.' Another time you put it this way, It's all part of the exciting adventure, the celebration that is life.'"

"Then you said how we can attain it." He looked up and smiled.

"By being one with where you are and who you are. Being aware of your feelings and emotions and doing things so you control them, so they don't control you."

Ben looked up all perky. "That was all that stuff you told us about recognizing thoughts when they come in and letting them go, especially negative ones. You also said that we will be surprised how many of our thoughts will be negative. You said that if we hold onto to them they can have power over us. That we need to replace them with positive thoughts, and this will shape us in a good way. And," Ben raised his voice excitedly, "Like when something happens in our lives, like when someone makes us mad or something, and we think of positive things we learned like, we are about peace, I am not a person of contention, and all that, and you feel better and aren't mad anymore, not following that path, not letting those feelings rule you."

"Wow," Angela said, sounding amazed by him.

Ben went on. "It's about being aware and being present, then we are one with our world and with ourselves."

Ben flipped some pages in his book of notes. "You taught to expand your mind and challenge it, through reading, to grow yourself, expand who you are, and then use it for the world."

"I have a lot more. Is it okay if I read you a little more?"

"Sure," Angela said, "You take great notes."

"So, our goal is to be constantly working on improving, in a state of growth so we can reach our given potential and then we'll go and live that to the world, and make a difference. We all have an incredible potential and we can't let it go to waste. You said much of the excitement about life comes from seeing that we each have special gifts, and a special thing to bring to the world, it's our own adventure, and only we can do it, as we were meant to. Gives our lives a unique purpose."

Angela nodded. "Yeah, awesome."

"We become aware of our thoughts, and don't hold onto the negative ones, we let them go and we reflect on positive thoughts that will help us grow. It's part of our striving for harmony within ourselves and then with our world around us, like I read before. We gain harmony with our environment by stopping and really noticing it, reflecting on what we see, and getting rid of any hindrances to that so it's just you and what you're perceiving. This is part of that necessary relationship between us and our world."

Ben continued reading and looking through his notebook. "And here's something we just talked about the other day. Don't worry about things you can't control, you will get where you need to go. The universe will move as it will, you can't control that. But it does interact with your actions." He looked up, "You told me to trust in the fact that all things will ultimately happen as they are supposed to but we can greatly influence that with our thoughts and actions. You also told us of the importance of prayer, and recognizing something bigger than us, way beyond us, and how that should give us comfort. Also, you said we should ask for the things we need, like being able to let go of fear, to have strength."

"I love this quote from you," he added, "You have to use these disciplines to fight through the shroud of fear that blocks us from realizing and creating and making our dreams happen, and living the free, unhindered life that we would love."

"I would love to do that," he said.

"You can. It's up to you," Angela said.

"Thanks." Ben looked pleased but then looked down and it seemed that something was bothering him.

"Something bugging you buddy?" Angela said softly."

Ben turned away a bit, hiding his face. He turned back and tossed his notebook down onto the blanket, looking down.

"What's the matter?"

Ben looked embarrassed. He hesitated, looking pained to speak. "I just..." He looked right at Angela. "I write all this stuff and I'm nothing like it."

"What do you mean?" Angela said.

"I'm not like you at all, I can't do what you do, be like you."

"I like who **you** are," Angela said.

Ben looked embarrassed from his admission, "I shouldn't have said anything." He started to get up to leave.

"Don't feel that way, I'm your friend, I care about you." Angela put her hand down on the grass, gesturing for him to sit. "I have my own stuff and I need friends to talk to about it also."

Ben sat back down and looked more calm. "It's just, I mean...I could never do the stuff you do...I feel like a coward."

Ben pulled up some grass and threw it, looking away. "I couldn't lead a protest like you did, and rally everyone not to fear the cops when they came. I never could have rescued Em the way you did."

Then it was quiet, the only sounds coming from the other kids in the distance milling around the campus.

"Maybe that's why I like "Lord of the Rings" so much, because all of the main characters are so brave and stuff."

"Hey," Angela said softly, "We are all here to do different things. You're not supposed to do what I do. You are here to fulfill your own special purpose, with your own unique set of gifts, your own adventure." Angela looked up and then at Ben, "And you're the only one who can do that."

He looked at Angela.

"Yeah, only you," she said.

"And we love you for who you are. We are here to fulfill our own destinies."

They both then looked out at the beautiful day, and two kids throwing a Frisbee some distance away.

"And," Angela said, more energetically, "Lord of the Rings is a great analogy for it."

"Think so huh?"

"Yeah man. It's all about what we are talking about. Becoming the person you are meant to be, growing, overcoming fear, the essential nature of the environment, especially trees, saving the world. Oh yeah."

"But they were all so brave. Even in my own destiny, how am I going to do that?" Ben looked away as he did before. "I'm a wimp who hides in stories."

"No you're not. No way, I've known you long enough to know that's totally not true. And I love that story, it's one of the best ever, and there are so many awesome analogies of life in it."

She smiled at him as if she just thought of something.

"What?" Ben said.

"I loved Galadrial," Angela said.

"Me too," Ben said.

"I love that part where she bids them farewell on their journey to Mordor. And she gives them gifts and encouragement. It's so beautiful and ethereal, just like her."

"I love that part," Ben said.

"It's so great, Angela went on, the book deals with many of the main characters dealing with fear, with finding courage. And when you read it and see that they do, you're so inspired by it, your soul rises, feel like taking on the world."

Ben smiled.

They sat for another minute silently. Then Angela looked at him.

"I wonder if people will ever say, Let's hear about Frodo and the ring. And they'll say, Yes, that's one of my favorite stories. Frodo was really courageous wasn't he, Dad? Yes, m'boy, the most famousest of Hobbits. And that's saying a lot.'"

Angela looked intently at Ben and smiled. "Now it's your turn. Write your own story"

"How?"

"Live your life as we always say, following your path, eyes wide open, living fully in the moment, with abandon. Let it come and let it go, you're flowing with it and feeling free. And..."

She paused, smiling at him.

"And?" Ben asked.

"You will find your courage."

Ben smiled as if he wished he could believe it.

"You will. Just go with it. We are all in the process of growth. Be at peace, just be you, and you'll do what you need to. Look how great you've been doing since I've known you. You certainly won us over."

"Thanks."

"It's true. And that's what friends do for each other."

Just then Emily and a friend sat down and joined them.

"Hey, Anita was looking for you." Emily said. "Says she has something to tell you. She looked excited."

"Huh," Angela said. "I'll go see, thanks."
Angela left them sitting there and went to the office.

When she got there Anita was excited, practically jumping up and down when she told Angela the news she had. "Hey, our town's university wants you to speak at their big rally coming up."

"Me?" Angela said. "Why?

"They are very impressed with things you've been doing young lady. You've been on the national news twice this year, you know."

Angela put her hand on her forehead, "Oh brother."

"This is huge that they asked you. And I'm so proud of you." Anita grabbed Angela's shoulders.

"Oh man, I don't know." Angela said skeptically.

"Don't know? Man you have to do this. You have great things to say and people need to hear it. And I'm going to be there front row and center to see it. There's even a rumor that your hero Dr. King will be there! Can you believe it?"
Angela's eyes got wide.

"Yeeeahh, how about that!" Anita added.

"I'll have to think about that." Angela said.

"Think about it?!"

A student in the office interrupted Anita to ask her what today's date was. Anita walked over to the desk where he was filling something out.

"April 8th," Anita said.

"What's the year again?" He asked.

"My goodness young man," Anita said, "You don't even know what year it is, sheeesh. 1968. April 8th, 1968."

At that moment Angela had no idea the events of this date would stay with her all of her life, without diminishing.

13

For the Person She Held in the Highest Esteem

The news that came that day, hit Angela deeper than she ever experienced in her life. She was in her room after eating dinner early by herself as her mother was away visiting her sister. The show she was watching in the background as she sat at her desk was interrupted as the awful news was broadcast. Angela turned to face the large black and white television on her floor. She was totally shocked by what she heard. She stood eyes still fixed on the television set. Dr. Martin Luther King had been assassinated. As it sank into her mind, the reality setting in, she felt herself drop to her knees and cry.

She doesn't know how long she was there, but woke up several hours later laying on her side and the room was dark except for the bright gray glow from the screen. She turned off the set. Then stood looking out of her window, the lights from the neighbor's houses in the distance the only thing she could see. She walked closer to her window and looked out. She thought of how she had always looked out from there, always from that same window of all she had in her room, and in that same spot just as she had done since being a little girl. She couldn't understand the comfort she obtained from peering out into the glow of the lights at night from that spot, but felt some of the comfort now, feeling like she badly needed the security of it, and a reminder of simpler times.

Her lifelong hero had been taken from the world. The person she admired most was not here anymore. Strength tempered by love, she thought. How peaceful he was in the face of such hatred. He wanted to change the world for the better just as she did. She felt as though she drew strength from him. She stayed by the window, in her favorite spot, watching the glow from the lights in her neighborhood.

When Angela left the spot by the window she sat on the floor against her bed and went into a time of prayer and mediation. She sat there all night and all of the next day, breaking from it only when she had to. She wanted to pay homage to her hero and pray for his family to be comforted and cared for, and that the world would not forget what he said, but that his message would be strengthened.

She also needed to prepare her mind to be able to meet the challenges that lay ahead in light of this. She wanted to do all she could for the world and asked for the strength to do that. She wanted to be prepared to function as she needed to, and care for the people put in her path. This event was so life shattering; she automatically went into this time without thinking about it.

When she went back to school she went straight to the office and told Anita that she would definitely be speaking at the rally at the university. She found that Anita's attitude had completely changed since the assassination.

'There is so much paranoia going on right now." Anita said. Everybody's freakin' out. The rally is still planned to go but they're not sure about security. They are trying to get it together in time. Some people, key leaders have pulled out. You should definitely not risk even going over here. The way things are going…"

Angela interrupted Anita, "I'm going."

"What!? Anita turned to follow Angela who was walking out of the office.

Anita grabbed Angela. "Stop!" She turned Angela around. "You can't be serious. There is a reason other speakers, key leaders have pulled out." Anita turned as if to tell everyone in the office and was flailing her arms as she spoke. "Some of the speakers have received death threats and the university has been getting death threats called in and…"

Angela interrupted her again, gently holding Anita's shoulders to keep her from excitedly flailing around. "I have to go. If we back down all is lost, we can't cave in and let the people who threaten us decide which way the country goes. The country needs leaders to stand up, not run away."

"No!" Anita insisted.

Angela held on and gently shook Anita's shoulders and looked in her eyes to assure her. "It will be alright. I know this is what I'm supposed to do."

Getting shot?! Who's suppoooosed to get shot?

Angela laughed. I don't know what's going to happen to me, I don't think about that. That's not up to me." Angela dropped her voice to a whisper. "But, I know what I'm supposed to do."

Anita looked at her in disbelief. She dropped her pen on the floor and turned to go back to her desk in the office shaking her head.

"Don't worry," Angela called to her as she opened the office door to leave, but there was no response.

Shonice was in the hall walking up to the office. "What's going on? I could hear Anita yelling all the way down here."

"She's all upset that I'm still going to speak at the rally."

"You're going?"

"Yeah, I have to go."

"Why?" Shonice asked. "And after all that's happened?"

"Now more than ever people need encouragement," Angela said. "And that comes from courage."

"Some of their major headline speakers they had lined up have pulled out, they were getting death threats." Shonice told her, looking concerned.

"I know. More reason than ever to go."

"People will tell you you're crazy." Shonice said.

"I've heard that before plenty of times and sometimes that can be the best confirmation you're on the right track."

Shonice laughed.

As they started walking down the hall toward class, Ethan was hurriedly trying to make his way through the crowd of students to get to them. He was out of breath when he got there. "Hey Shonice." He said.

"Hey."

His face changed to a serious look when he looked at Angela. "Ang, you can't go the rally, it's way too dangerous." Angela looked at Shonice as Ethan went on not even noticing. Key speakers have dropped out, the university is getting death threats, and from what I've heard the whole thing is in disarray organization wise." He paused to breathe.

"I'm going." Angela calmly told him.

"What!?" Ethan was shocked that she was going. "Why?"

"Because the people need someone to stand up, not walk away."

"Not like this, this makes no sense!" Ethan fired back, looking more upset.

"I have to go to class." She told him and Angela and Shonice started walking to their class together.

"This is crazy!" Ethan gestured to them as they were walking though the crowd to class.

"We'll talk about this later." Ethan called out.

Angela turned calmly. "There's nothing to talk about. I know I need to go."

Ethan held both hands on his head. "I don't believe this!"

"Is this our first fight?" She said wryly. And then ran up quickly as Ethan stood expressionless, and kissed him, and then ran to Shonice to head to class.

Shonice stopped Angela after class, as they were standing in a quieter part of the hallway where there were no other students.

"Hey, I wanted to talk to you about the rally." Shonice said concerned.

"Sure, what?"

"This has nothing to do with Ethan or Anita, or anybody else."

"What?"

'I'm worried about you going, don't think it's a good idea."

Shonice held her hand up. "I know all the, 'I gotta do all this for mankind…and all that, I got that." Shonice said.

Then her expression turned more serious. "But I am really concerned about you going."

Before Angela could say anything. Shonice added,

"That's why I'm coming with you."

Angela looked up surprised.

"Yes, I know there is no way I am going to be able to convince you not to, so there's no way you're going without me." Shonice added.

Angela seemed to want to say something but couldn't. She looked endearingly at her.

Angela walked closer and placed her hands on the sides of Shonice's face. "We can't back down from things like this, can't slow down, can't cower, while our world is still judging people simply by the color of their skin."

Angela took her hands down, thinking hard about what she just said, and shook her head slowly back and forth.

"Not as long as that still goes on," Angela added, "no one can."

Angela knelt down to grab her backpack, threw it over her shoulder, and started to head the other way to her class, then stopped and turned.

"I'm honored, Shonice Harriet Williamson, that you're my friend.

14

For the People
The Rally

The media showed up at Angela's school two days after word was out that Angela planned on speaking at the rally. It became a major story due to the fact that not on was she still planning on going, but how she talked of courage and not letting threats decide the fate of the country, and how the people need leadership in spite of danger, gained national attention. It was known that major speakers slated to appear had withdrawn due to personal death threats as well as threats called into the university. Angela's stance was so striking due to the fa that she said all of the events since Dr. King's untimely death motivated her more, much more, to be sure to go.

Her words of conviction resonated strongly with many people. They felt she was indeed concerned for them, wanted them to have hope, and had a positive vision for individual people and the world. The people were fallin in love with her message, her courage, and her caring fc them, even at the expense of her life.

Each time the news captured another milestone moment in her life such as the protest march, the groups of peop hearing her message and then bursting out in celebratio with the song, "Let's work together," The beach event with the sunrise, and now the rally, was causing a powerful wave of interest and fascination with this remarkable young woman. Angela had also become a h news story, one that people always wanted to watch. Th media had been looking more deeply into her life upon her popularity and had discovered the stories about her rescuing her friend, the butterflies and their release whe she was a little girl and the "Age of Aquarius" incident.

People wanted to meet her more than ever now and hear her strong message of hope and peace.

Three news vans pulled up to the school to be positioned there for the end of school so they could interview Angela before she left. The principal called her out of class when they alerted him of their coming.

Angela went up to the school's office. The principal, Mr. Blum was standing holding his door open, a blank look on his face. Angela went in. The principal closed the door and sat down.

"Have a seat," He said gesturing.

He let out a breath as he sat down, looking tense.

"You're causing quite a stir," He said.

"How so sir?" Angela asked.

"There are three news vans outside this school right now," He said pointing to the wall. "And they all want to interview you, young lady."

'Why would they want to do that?" Angela asked innocently.

He blew out a breath and sat back hard in his chair.

"Because,...Of your speaking at the rally."

I was asked to." Angela answered softly.

"That, for starters, I don't understand in the slightest. It's a national event. Whose idea was that?" He puffed. "You're just a kid, this is way out of your league young lady."

"I still don't understand why I am here?"

Mr. Blum was looking increasingly frustrated, his true feelings coming out.

"Because," he said with more emphasis, "You have continually caused disruptions in this school, and now it's going over the top."

"I'm sorry," Angela answered "I don't see where I've caused disruptions, honestly."

Mr. Blum's face and head turned red. "You have, repeatedly." He said.

"But sir, a disruption implies trouble, interference. I don't see where I have done any of that here."

He sat back hard again, unable to formulate a response, not expecting her remark.

"Don't get smart with me young lady," His voice rose. "I run this school, not you."

Everyone in the outer office could hear him including several news reporters who were up there waiting to discuss the interview. They looked at each other.

"And I will not have some fanatical female student lead it around by the nose."

"Sir, with all due respect, I have done none of those things, nor would I ever want to."

"Don't with all due respect me, you led a major district wide walk-out, you don't call that a disruption?!" He stood up, red-faced. "I voted to have you expelled, but couldn't get enough votes on my side because too many people are afraid of the public and the press. But I've got news for you, in this school I'm in charge!"

The reporters outside the door looked indignant after hearing his remark. One of them started writing on his notepad.

He walked around from his desk. "And now you are going to go marching off to this rally, which shouldn't be allowed anyway, a bunch of hippie subversives!"

"This is inappropriate. I'm leaving." Angela got up and started walking out.

The principal stormed over as she began opening the door. They both were in plain view of everyone in the office, including the reporters whose expressions toward him spoke volumes. The principal's face went from red to pale.

Angela walked out calmly, and the reporters approached her. Mr. Blum closed the door behind him, trying to hide his face.

The reporters arranged to interview Angela on the steps in front of the school. When everything was ready they started asking her questions. They wanted to know why she decided to go. She told them how in a situation like this the people need a message of hope and encouragement.

The rest of the interview went well. She was glad becaus she was upset how Mr. Blum treated her and wasn't sure if she could pull herself together so quickly.

The day of the rally came. The local news had been talking all day about it. The media was everywhere, vans and reporters and camera men were walking all around wading through the crowds. There was a much bigger crowd than expected probably due to all the publicity surrounding the major speakers dropping out and Angela's rising popularity. Security looked insufficient for the size of the crowd, and more people were coming every minute.

The scene looked confusing as Angela pulled up in her VW Bus with Shonice and Ben and Emily. They drove past where the crowds were parking and eventually a police officer for the University stopped them. It was noisy when Angela rolled her window down to speak with him.

"You can't be here," he said over the noise.

"I'm a speaker," Angela said.

He looked her over, and then looked past her into the bus

Someone who was with him recognized Angela. "Let them through, that's Angela."

As they started to pull forward Shonice smiled at Angela from the passenger seat in front.

"That's Angela," She said, still smiling.

"Stop it." Angela said as she turned the wheel. Ben and Emily both laughed in the back.

They were directed to an area to park. When they stopped the car, they all looked out. They all sat without saying anything, taken by the magnitude of the size of the crowd.

"Whoa." Ben said with a long breath.

The hills all around where they were parked were teaming with people, and it had an air of intensity and foreboding, the crowds outnumbering the security by too great a number.

Up to this point no one in the VW Bus had yet said anything, everyone was still staring out all around through the windows of the bus, feeling safer inside and not looking anxious to leave.

Angela sat with them looking out.

Then sensing it, said. "Let's go," and opened her door.

Angela had on an outfit with its usual flair and bright colors; pants with alternating stripes of brown, orange and yellow running down, a long sleeved white top with ruffles and puffed sleeves and boots. She was also wearing a necklace with a large peace sign medallion, and small, round, dark blue sunglasses with metal rims.

She walked out confidently. There was no pretentiousness in her at all, what she exuded was simply part of who she was naturally, there was no agenda in it. As she strode out toward the crowds after coming out of the bus you felt the power that emanated from her spirit. People noticed her instantly, many knew who she was and were moving toward her. If they didn't know who she was they sensed something special about her and were drawn over as well. Before they had gone far a crowd was around her. The four looked around surprised.

"Man," Shonice said stupefied. "This is wild."

All three friends moved to stand between Angela and the crowd. She stood behind them as the throng of people were all calling things out at once. Shonice began walking ahead and moving the people out of the way.

"She can't talk now, she's got to go."

Shonice deftly moved them through the mob, people responding well to her, as she kept Angela safe, directly behind her. As they were making their way through the crowd members of the press saw her and closed in on the group of friends. Angela answered the questions as people were swarmed around her.

There was so much excitement surrounding her, her notoriety had been building feverishly recently and the timing was ripe for it as the people seemed in desperate need of something positive to cling to. She was all that and more, the crowd growing in excitement around her. But it began to give them all an uneasy feeling, especially Shonice who was in control and stayed in front of Angela and began to lead them all out. Telling the press she had to go, Shonice decided to lead them to the stage area ahead of them, up the hill.

The four made their way up to the large stage area which was a temporary one set up on the huge grass area of the University's great lawn. No one had been there to greet them, they had to make their way themselves. When they were up and behind the stage, they all looked relieved.

"Thanks," Angela said to Shonice, a bit out of breath.

Shonice looked back out at the crowd. "Man, you're like a rock star girl! This is crazy."

"Crazy is right," Angela agreed.

'Where is everybody?" Emily asked looking around.

Finally they saw someone they could talk to. There were two young men who seemed to be in charge. One was tall and had a long pony tail tied tightly back. He held a clipboard and approached Angela.

"Are you Angela?" He asked, presuming it was her.

169

"Yes," she said.

"Ready?" He asked her.

"Yes," Angela answered.

He looked her over. "Is that all you have?" Surprised she didn't have any notes of any kind.

"Yup," Angela said confidently, moving her arms, "Just me."

The man remained serious and looked preoccupied. He stepped away for a few minutes, talking with two other young guys.

He walked back over to Angela. "Would you be willing to be our keynote speaker?" He asked her.

"Keynote?"

"Our headliner, giving the major address. Everyone else is giving short, 5 minute speeches. The keynote as you know is the headliner, the featured speaker. They talk for 15-20 minutes as the main message. It's the one everyone is really here for."

Angela looked out the crowd, stunned and amazed by his request, feeling a wave of nervousness rush through her. Then looked back as him. "Yes, I will."

"Great," he said, and left quickly, leaving the friends standing there together.

They all stood together silently. Shonice put her hands on Angela's shoulder and smiled. "Damn!" She turned and looked at the crowd. "You're going to be great."

Ben walked up to her and rested his head on her shoulder. "I'm glad that you are you. And not me," he added.

A few minutes later Angela moved out on stage further toward the front not really thinking about it. People started to see her and recognize her. They began yelling shouts of praise and encouragement out to her. She felt the powerful presence of the crowd's excitement and the uneasiness that accompanied it and started walking backwards toward the back of the stage.

Angela and her friends sat with the other speakers who were there in a small area backstage. It was on the top of a hill and walled off at the back with a curtain at the front so it afforded them some level of privacy from the large crowd.

Angela felt more nervous as the first speaker went on, but quickly reminded herself of why she was there and the purpose of it. This was much bigger than her, she told herself. This was not about her, and kept repeating it in her mind. She felt calmer and definitely focused. She kept focusing herself on why she was there. To carry on the work of her hero and to give people the message of acting for change in our world and unifying everyone in peace. As she spoke to herself she began to get more excited to speak, her nervousness and intimidation over the huge tumultuous crowd diminishing.

Although several speakers had opted out, there were still some fairly well known people there, people she read about, and she could not believe she was on the same stage as them. Things were moving along smoothly, the crowd reacting well to the speakers, and remaining in control. This surprised her just because of the sheer number of people, she found it hard not to believe that such a number of people would not be even louder. Then, there was a disturbance and someone had to be taken away. His anger and hatred toward the speaker unnerving. He flailed wildly as they carted him away, several men needed to do it.

Emily looked at her nervously, never seeing anyone acting like that before. He looked as though he definitely would have killed the man who was speaking on the stage if they didn't grab him. Angela could see Emily looked shaken and put one arm around her.

The crowd remained contained since the man who caused the disturbance had been carted away, Angela thought, only getting really loud when they introduced the speakers and occasionally as they spoke.

Finally, it was Angela's turn. There was a longer break than normal between speakers for her. And it turned out her introduction would be longer also. She felt sad at this moment that Ethan wasn't there. They had not spoken since the time Ethan got so upset in the main hall of their school. They hadn't spoken largely due to the fact that they never had a chance to talk and she had been so busy. It bothered her thinking about them being at odds and not having reconciled. She felt like much of his reaction was

ased on his surprise that she was still going after all of
ne press about the danger involved.

ight before her introduction someone ran up to her and
anded her a letter. It was from Ethan. Somehow he had
smuggled up to her, and the timing could not have been
nore perfect. She wanted to be at her absolute best to
ave the biggest impact on the people and truly affect
hange, and this was just what she needed. She heard his
oice in her head as she read it quickly knowing she
idn't have much time.

*Ang. I care deeply for you and I'm so sorry, I should not
ave doubted your calling to do what you're doing, or
our conviction to stand for the people even when others
n. Go get em' kiddo, light up the world as only you can,
nd move it toward great changes. You were brought into
is world to make a strong and positive difference, your
ecial purpose. The people need you, I need you, and the
orld needs you. Light it on fire! Love Ethan."*

ast as she finished reading the letter she heard her name
alled.

he crowd exploded when they saw her. The wave of
neers and applause hit her like a huge wall. She stood
ill for a second shocked by it. She regained composure
nd remembered again why she was there. She walked up
the microphone.

Thank you. I'm glad to see all of you here."

here were loud cheers and she had to wait.

"We are here..." She said and then paused and looked at all of them.

"We are here. No matter what anyone feared would happen, no matter how many said not to come, we are here.

You know **why** we're here?"

She grabbed the microphone off the stand and walked to the edge of the stage.

"You know **why** we're here?!" She said louder.

The crowd roared a unanimous explosion of "Yes!!"

"We're here because we care about this country." Loud cheers followed her words.

"We care about our world," She said raising her voice again.

"We know..." She tried to go on but the crowed was too loud for her to be heard.

She started again. "We're here because we believe peace is possible."

She started walking the length of the stage. "We're here because we know that people have the capacity, the potential, to live in harmony, to live in love, to live in peace.

We're here…"

She paused, letting her words hang powerfully in the air.

"Because we are not going to be scared away from proclaiming that, to all the world."

There was a long series of cheers.

"We're here because we want our leaders to hear us."

The crowd noise grew deafening. She backed up a few steps knowing she had to wait a bit.

"We want our leaders to know that we will not stand for unjust wars. That we will not tolerate people being marginalized because of the color of their skin. If we don't quit…We will prevail."

Applause broke out for a solid thirty seconds. People were still whistling and shouting approvingly.

"But we must do this peacefully and thoughtfully." She added.

'I love my country," Angela said more softly. The crowd getting quieter, not expecting to hear that.

'This country has the greatest system in the world. That's why I am **able** to be here."

She walked over to the edge of the stage again and pointed to the whole crowd.

"That's why you're **able** to be here!

"But..." She paused again, looking out at the crowd.

"But, if we don't get very involved, and...if we don't speak our minds, we could lose it all, and...it won't be great anymore."

Cheers erupted again.

When the crowd died down enough for her to speak again she added, "That's why we **had** to be here."

Angela went on describing how exactly to get involved, and who to contact and what we need to constantly be telling them. And to never quit no matter what and it will work. She kept telling them that you are the hammer that drives the nail, that you really have the power, and we have to use it for good.

It came time for her to close her speech.

"Now, most importantly, love...people. Love everybody! But don't leave here and talk about what a great speech it was and then go on not loving people, that is nothing. Then...you might as well not have come today."

She stood and looked at the crowd for emphasis.

"Make this impact you, for good. You are going to make a life commitment to love people. I don't care if they make you mad, I don't care if they have long hair, or...if they have short hair, or...if they are black,...or white,…or green! Love them." She said throwing her hands up.

Cheers abounded, and whistles, and applause.

When she could speak again she added, "If we do this, and we don't stop….We will change the world,…one person at a time. Thank you!"

The crowd was deafening. People were pounding on the stage. They started lining up on one side of the stage where the stairs were to meet Angela. She wanted to reach the crowd on a personal level so she went over where they were piling up to meet her. She bent to shake their hands and then stepped down on the ladder on the stage a few steps to get closer.

Shonice, Emily and Ben all ran over to where Angela was knee deep in the crowd. Ben climbed down first so he could be right alongside her. People were shaking hands with her and many were talking with her loudly and cheerfully. Everyone was laughing and having a good time.

A contrasting series of shouts from one person suddenly shattered the din of all the laughter and joy. It contrasted harshly and got everyone's attention quickly. A man was shouting up at the stage at Angela and it seemed like for a moment that it was all anyone could hear, until screams and shrieks also filled the air as he drew a gun and pointed it at Angela. Emily screamed seeing him point it at her, his face filed with hate. Ben saw him as well in that terrible second of time that seemed like an eternity.

There was a loud bang as the gun went off but Ben had already thrown himself over Angela, covering her with his back. The bullet hit Ben. You could hear screaming in the crowd. The people bravely knocked the man immediately to the ground and disarmed him, holding him down, piling on him as he shouted and tried to get out, until the police could get over to him.

Dazed, Angela turned around and saw that she was surprisingly alive but then saw Ben falling over, his back covered in blood. She grabbed him reflexively and held him, and with the help of several others got him on the stage and gently laid him down on his stomach. Angela asked a fan for his shirt so she could try and stop the bleeding. He pulled off his T-shirt and Angela balled it up and held it against the wound. A person from the crowd who turned out to be a fellow student at their school, Joel Murphy, had the where with all to grab the microphone, which thank goodness was still on and began calling out. A man has been shot, he is on the stage, please get an ambulance up here.

He kept repeating that message, until the police and an ambulance got there, as Angela, Shonice, Emily and concerned fans crowded around Ben in an eerily surreal moment. There was a cacophony of sounds all blending disturbingly together as they waited; screams of horror, crying, people yelling for help, cries in frustration for how long it was taking.

Angela clung to her friend, holding the blood soaked shirt over the wound trying to keep his blood from running out. "C'mon buddy, hang on, hang in there buddy." Her voice was mixed with tears as she kept speaking to him. "We're going to get through this buddy, we will, you're going to be alright, buddy, you're going to be alright."

People that were around her, hearing her talk to him, were crying as she did, looking sad, and shocked, all thinking he would be dead in minutes. It seemed like too much time had gone by and many had lost hope and watched despondently as Angela held him, her clothes now covered in blood as well.

Finally, an ambulance siren and police siren could be heard together coming through the grassy area toward the stage. The people were all moving as fast as they could to get out of the way. All the while the people still held the suspect, having bound him with whatever they could find. The police car followed the ambulance, the people trying to make room for them to approach. It was frustrating as they approached how they slowed due to the crowd. All of Ben's closest friends huddled around him watching the ambulance try to get through the thick crowd near the stage.

Finally they were there and paramedics ran toward the stage, equipment in hand. All the while the police were handcuffing the man who fired the shot, who was trying to turn his head so he could see what was happening on the stage, but was turned around to be placed in the car, the same angry look in his face.

The paramedics worked on Ben and finally he was loaded into the ambulance to go to the hospital. Angela would not leave his side and sternly insisted to the men that she was going. They looked at each other not knowing what to do and closed the door with Angela inside. Shonice drove the VW bus to the hospital with Emily to meet them there.

When they arrived at the hospital, Emily followed Shonice into the emergency entrance, where they eventually saw Angela standing by the doors to the operating room, still in the same clothes stained with Ben's blood. Shonice ran over and hugged her. Other kids from their school who were at the rally eventually came in and saw them and also ran over. Everyone crowded around her and hugged her as a group.

"What's going on?" Shonice asked.

"The paramedics slowed the bleeding way down, they did what they could in the ambulance." Angela moved away from the operating room entrance. Her face wet with tears. Shonice gently held her shoulders and led her away from the door. She brought her over to the chairs and helped her sit down. Everyone crowded around in support, Shonice sat in the chair right next to her.

"How is he?" She asked softly.

"Don't know, he's bad." She looked up at the ceiling. "He lost a lot of blood."

Just then Ethan came running down the hall and knelt down in front of Angela. "You okay?" He said excitedly.

"Yes," she said.

"It's Ben." Shonice said.

"What?" Ethan asked.

"Yeah," Shonice went on, "The brave little guy, jumped in front, covered Ang and took the bullet."

Angela whispered something.

"What honey?" Ethan said gently.

"He found his courage."

"What?" Ethan said softly, not understanding.

Angela waved her hand, preoccupied with Ben's condition.

"I'll explain later." And she put her hand gently on Ethan's shoulder in front of her still kneeling.

After four hours of waiting, a doctor came up to where Angela and members of Ben's family were sitting. He looked tired and his gown was soaked with sweat. He spoke to Ben's mother and father. "He is going to be alright."

"Oh, thank God," His mother said, covering her mouth.

The bullet went in, hit a rib, and lodged there. We got it out, no major organs were hit. He was very lucky. We want to keep him here and under observation tonight, if he continues as we expect, he'll be moved to a regular room tomorrow and you can see him then."

The doctor turned and looked at Angela. "You two saved each other. That bullet might have killed you if he didn't jump in front of it, and he would have bled to death if you didn't cover the wound like you did."

The next day only Ben's parents were allowed in to see him. He was still in critical care but improving. Everyone was very anxious to see him but had to wait another day when they moved him to his own room. Angela was the last one of the gang from school to see him because she couldn't be there right after school as everyone had. She went up as soon as she could, and when she rounded the corner on the floor he was on she could see Ben lying on his bed just staring. She stopped for a second, smiled, and walked into his room.

"Hey buddy," she said softly. "How are you?"

Ben smiled. "Fine."

Angela pulled a chair up to the bed and sat by him. She put her hand on his.

"I am so glad you're alive."

"Me too," he said. And they both laughed.

"Thanks," Angela said.

Ben waved his hand as if it was nothing.

"You were awesome." Angela said.

She reached into her pocket and pulled out a small cloth pouch with a pull tie at the top.

"I got you this."

"What is it?" Ben tried to sit up more but couldn't move, and let out a groan.

"Don't try to move, your rib remember?"

"I do now," Ben grunted.

Angela laughed.

Ben opened the small pouch and pulled out a ring. He held it up, turning it slowly as he looked at it "Wow, what's this?"

Then he figured it out. "It's Aragorn's ring," He said smiling. He kept looking it over. "Man, why this?"

Angela smiled at him, not saying anything. Ben took his eyes off the ring and looked at her.

"Because, Peregrin Took...you found your courage." Angela said with a big smile.

Ben paused, in thought about what she said. His face lit up when he remembered back to the conversation they had on courage that day outside.

He smiled at Angela. "I guess so huh?"

He put it on his finger. "Why Aragorn's?"

"Because he was the biggest hero of the story."

Ben looked thoughtful. "I don't know, you could argue Frodo…"

Angela cut him off and put her hand on his. "Shhhh."

She gently patted his hand. "I wouldn't be here if it wasn't for you."

"That's what heroes do," Ben answered jokingly.

"They sure do buddy." Angela agreed. "They sure do."

15

To the Next Adventure

When Angela turned her VW Bus from the road onto the short gravel road leading up to her house she saw Ethan standing at the steps holding a bouquet of flowers. She parked alongside the house and got out.

"Wellllll, wow." She said as she walked up to him. She looked at the flowers and smiled.

"Man. You must really love flowers to walk around holding them."

"They're for you," He said, handing them to her.

"Oooo, beautiful. I love them." She held them up and smelled them. "Ahh, Wonderful. Thanks."

"I have something else for you." Ethan said.

Angela smiled. "Oh?"

Ethan let out a short laugh over how she said it.

"You're cute," He said.

"I'm cute?" Angela said moving closer, looking up at him.

"Yes," Ethan said. He pulled something out of his pocket. "And I wondered if you would wear this?" And he held up a ring.

Angela moved her head back slightly to see, then looked back up at Ethan. She looked at him, mouth opened, silent. She took a deep breath.

"I want you to have it." Ethan paused, and looked at her, his eyes full of expression.

Angela took the ring and held it.

"I want us to go out," Ethan said. "If you'll have me."

She loved the way he said it. Angela placed the ring on her finger. "Yes,"

"Yeah?" Ethan said, a lilt in his voice.

"Oh yeah." Angela said.

Ethan hugged her tight and lifted her up. When he put her back down, they looked at each other again, and he slowly moved forward and kissed her. They hugged, the ring glistening on her hand.

31664383R00106

Made in the USA
San Bernardino, CA
16 March 2016